ADAM HAMILTON'S

24 HOURS
That Changed the World

For Younger Children

Jesus'
Last Week on Earth

DAPHNA FLEGAL

Abingdon Press
Nashville

24 HOURS
That Changed the World
For Younger Children
Jesus' Last Week on Earth

Art Credits: p. 5: Barbara Ball © 1998 Cokesbury; pp. 9, 39, 49: Robert S. Jones © 1998 Abingdon Press; p. 12: Megan Jeffery © 1999 Abingdon Press; p. 19: Megan Jeffery © 2000 Abingdon Press; p. 22: (foot): Florence Davis © 2010 Cokesbury; p. 22: (bowl and towel) Brenda Gilliam © 2003 Abingdon Press; pp. 29, 59: Robert S. Jones © 2000 Abingdon Press; p. 32: Florence Davis © 2001 Abingdon Press; p. 45: Gillian Chapman/Linden Artists © 2002 Cokesbury; p. 52: (rooster outline) Keitha Vincent © 2009 Cokesbury; p. 56: Megan Jeffery © 2001 Cokesbury; p. 62: Barbara Upchurch © 2000 Cokesbury; p. 69: Megan Jeffery © 2003 Abingdon Press.

Daphna Flegal lives in Nashville, Tennessee, where she is a writer and editor of children's curriculum resources. She is a diaconal minister in the West Michigan Conference of The United Methodist Church, where she served in local congregations as Director of Children's Ministries and Director of Christian Education. She presently serves as lead editor for children's resources at The United Methodist Publishing House. She is excited about her newest job—grandmother!

ISBN 978-1-4267-1430-6

PACP00777822-01

10 11 12 13 14 15 16 17 18 19—10 9 8 7 6 5 4 3 2 1

Printed in the U. S. A.

CONTENTS

Your church can do a church-wide study of *24 Hours* by using the older children's resource, *24 Hours That Changed the World: Jesus' Last Week on Earth (For Older Children)* by Marcia Stoner; the youth resource, *24 Hours That Changed the World (For Youth)* by Jason Gant; and the adult resource, *24 Hours That Changed the World* by Adam Hamilton.

1 THE TRIUMPHAL ENTRY

<table>
<tr><td>

Objectives
The children will
- hear Mark 11:1-11;
- discover that Jesus rode a donkey into Jerusalem as a sign of peace;
- learn that Palm Sunday is a special day when we remember Jesus' triumphal entry;
- have the opportunity to praise God through Jesus and proclaim Jesus as the Messiah.

</td><td>

Bible Story
Mark 11:1-11: Jesus rides a donkey into Jerusalem. Many people went along in front and behind him, shouting and waving palm branches.

Bible Verse
Mark 11:9: Hosanna! Blessed is the one who comes in the name of the Lord!

</td></tr>
</table>

Focus for the Teacher

An Unexpected Messiah

For years and years the prophets had promised that God would send a Messiah to redeem the people of Israel. When Jesus entered the city riding a colt that had never been ridden, he was publicly announcing that he was that Messiah. His action fulfilled the prophecy Zechariah had written centuries before: "Lo, your king comes to you; triumphant and victorious is he, humble and riding on a donkey, on a colt, the foal of a donkey" (Zechariah 9:9).

> Hosanna! Blessed is the one who comes in the name of the Lord!
> Mark 11:9

It was traditional to cover the path of someone who was thought worthy of honor. When Jesus' followers welcomed him as he entered the city by spreading cloaks and palm branches on the road, they were giving Jesus the same honor they would give a king.

But for the many people who expected the Messiah to be more like a military leader, Jesus' entry into the city was a surprise. He did not enter on a horse as a conquering hero; rather, he entered riding a donkey, which was a symbol of humility and peace.

The Bible Verse

As the crowd of people went ahead and followed behind Jesus, they shouted, "Hosanna! Blessed is the one who comes in the name of the Lord!" The word *hosanna* is a plea for deliverance. It means "God will save" or "save us now." The people cried out for God to break in and save them. The scene was one of both messianic hope and misunderstanding of Jesus' role as Messiah. Many people were expecting the Messiah to end the oppression of Rome. Jesus wanted people to know that God's kingdom involves a new way of living.

Palm Sunday

Palm Sunday is celebrated the week before Easter and marks the beginning of Holy Week. This Sunday is also known as Passion Sunday, reminding us that in just a few short days the cries of "Hosanna!" changed to "Crucify him!" and Jesus was led to the cross.

For today's lesson we will concentrate on Palm Sunday. Children are often included in the church's celebration of Palm Sunday by waving palm branches, processing into worship, and singing. By including children in this celebration we show them that they are important in the worship life of the church.

Explore Interest Groups

Be sure that adult leaders are waiting when the first child arrives. Greet and welcome each child. Get the child involved in an activity that interests him or her and introduces the theme for the day's activities.

Palm Leaf Crosses

- Show the children a palm leaf.

- **Say:** In our Bible story today the people laid palm branches in the road as Jesus entered Jerusalem. These long, leafy branches grow from the top of the tall date palm. Palm leaves were a symbol of victory. By waving the palm branches and laying them in the road, the people would celebrate a conquering hero who they thought would save them. But Jesus was not a conquering hero. Jesus was the Messiah, a special king sent from God.

- Give each child a palm frond.

- Show each child how to fold the palm frond into a cross.

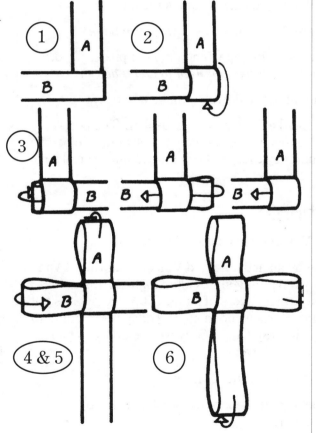

  1. Lay the ends of the two strips on top of each other as shown.

  2. Fold A down and then back around itself to make a loop around B.

  3. Fold B behind to the right and then through the center (A) to loop to the left.

  4. Slide A through the center in the back to make the top of the cross.

  5. Slide B through the center front to make the left side of the cross.

  6. Tuck the ends of A and B into the center to finish.

- If possible have the children make enough palm crosses to hand out to each person attending worship or each person participating in this study. The *24 Hours That Changed the World (for Older Children)* Leader's Guide

Prepare

✓ Photocopy the instructions (page 5) for each child.

✓ Provide: fresh, moist palm fronds, scissors

✓ Cut palm fronds into 14-inch lengths. You will need two strips per cross.

also suggests this activity so that enough crosses may be made. You may want to continue this activity in the next lessons until you have the number of crosses you need for the congregation.

adapted from ROCK SOLID: Middle Elementary, Leader's Guide, Spring 2010, © 2009 Cokesbury

Palm Leaf Poundings

- Show the children a palm leaf.

- **Say:** Palm trees were important to Bible-times life. Palm dates were eaten as a fruit. The palm leaves were used to make mats, brooms, ropes, baskets, and dishes. They were also used to build roofs and fences. Tree trunks were used to make lumber.

- Give each child a stack of newspapers to make a pad.

- Have each child arrange the leaves on the pads.

- Help the children carefully place the muslin or plain paper over the newspaper pads and leaves. Secure the muslin or paper with tape.

- Let the children gently pound the surface of the muslin or paper with a wooden mallet so that the color of the leaves comes through.

- Untape the muslin or paper and brush any leaves from the back.

- Weave a dowel through the slits at the top of each muslin piece. *(If you use plain paper instead of muslin, you will not need to add a dowel.)*

- Tie a length of yarn on each end of the dowel to make a hanger.

- **Say:** In our Bible story Jesus road a donkey into Jerusalem. The people laid palm branches on the road for the donkey to walk on. The people wanted to show Jesus that they thought he was someone special sent by God.

Impasto Palm Paintings

- Show the children a print of Vincent van Gogh's *Sunflowers*.

- **Say:** This painting was made by an artist named Vincent van Gogh. Van Gogh is known for using a painting style called *impasto*. Impasto is a kind of painting that uses thick layers of paint. Often the paint is put on the painting with a knife or a wooden stick. Today we're going to make impasto paintings like van Gogh. Only we are going to paint palm branches instead of sunflowers.

- Point out the vase of palm branches to the children.

- Have the children wear smocks, and prepare the work surface by covering the area with newspapers.

- Let the children help you mix the paint in disposable bowls. For each color mix one cup powdered tempera paint with two tablespoons wallpaper paste. Then add ⅓ cup liquid starch, and mix together until the mixture spreads easily. Green and yellow tempera paints will work for the palm branches. The third color should be the same as the vase you use.

Prepare

- ✓ Provide: palm leaves, wooden mallets, newspapers, unbleached muslin (or plain paper), masking tape, adult scissors, dowels, yarn

- ✓ Cut muslin into pieces, twelve to eighteen inches long. Fold down the top edge about two inches. Then cut 1-inch slits across the folded edge to create openings for a dowel to slide through.

Prepare

- ✓ Arrange real palm branches in a vase.

- ✓ Cover the work area with newspapers.

- ✓ Check your public library for books that have a print of *Sunflowers* by Vincent van Gogh. Or look online at: http://www.vangoghgallery.com/catalog/Painting/586/Still-Life:-Vase-with-Fifteen-Sunflowers.html.

NOTE: *Websites are constantly changing. Although these websites were checked at the time this book was edited, we recommend that you double check the site to verify that it is still live and that it is still appropriate for children before doing the activity.*

- ✓ Provide: heavy paper or cardboard, tempera paints, newspapers, smocks, craft sticks or plastic knives, disposable bowls, wallpaper paste, liquid starch, plastic mixing spoons, measuring cups and spoons

24 Hours That Changed the World (For Younger Children)

- Give each child a piece of heavy paper and a plastic knife or craft stick.

- Have the children spread the impasto mixture on the paper with the stick or knife. Encourage them to experiment with how thick they spread the paint.

- Set the paintings flat to dry.

- **Say:** In our Bible story today Jesus rides a donkey into the city of Jerusalem. As he entered, people were very excited.

- **Ask:** What makes you excited? What do you do when you are excited?

- **Say:** The people who saw Jesus waved palm branches and shouted, "Hosanna!" It was one way they showed Jesus that they thought he was someone special sent by God.

- Dispose of the paint mixture in the trash. Do **not** wash the paint down a sink.

A Game of Cloaks

- Show the children the Bible-times cloak or a picture of a cloak.

- **Say:** A cloak was very important in Bible times. In fact, a man could not enter the Temple unless he was wearing a cloak. A cloak protected its owner from the hot sun, sandstorms, and wind. It could even be used as a sleeping bag at night. Cloaks were long jackets made of woven cotton, wool, or flax and were dyed in many colors. Some cloaks had blue borders and fringes to remind people to obey God's commandments.

- Have the children choose a partner. One child will be player A, and the other child will be player B.

- Give each player A two pieces of fabric.

- **Say:** The people who heard Jesus was coming rushed out to greet him. They waved palm branches, and they put their cloaks on the road for the donkey to walk on. This was to show how much they honored Jesus. Let's find out how Jesus might have felt when he and the donkey walked across the cloaks.

- Point to the side of the room that you have designated as Jerusalem.

- Have the partners line up together on the opposite side of the room.

- **Say:** Player A will place one of the cloaks on the floor. Player B will step on it. Then player A will place the second cloak on the floor and player B will step on it, and so on until the partners reach Jerusalem. Listen carefully as you move to Jerusalem. When you hear me shout our Bible verse, "Hosanna! Blessed is the one who comes in the name of the Lord!" players A and B must switch duties.

- Shout, "Go!" to begin the game.

- Shout the Bible verse several times during the game.

adapted from PowerXpress! Triumphal Entry © 2002 Abingdon Press.

Prepare

✓ Provide: two pieces of fabric for each pair of children. Cut the fabric into squares or rectangles about 12-inches long

✓ Provide: a Bible-times cloak from your church's costume closet or a picture of a cloak. You may find an illustration of a cloak as well as other biblical clothing on the Internet at: http://www.womeninthe bible.net/3.3.Clothing_h ousing.htm

NOTE: *Websites are constantly changing. Although these websites were checked at the time this book was edited, we recommend that you double check the site to verify that it is still live and that it is still appropriate for children before doing the activity.*

Large Group

Bring all the children together to experience the Bible story. Clap two pieces of wood together to make the sound of donkey hooves to alert the children to the large group time. Use the transition activity to move the children from the interest groups to the large group area.

Palm Promenade

- Have the children move to an open area of the room.

- Divide the children into teams. Have teams line up on one side of the room.

- On the opposite side of the room, place the palm branch cards face down in piles for each team.

- Have the first person from each team run to the team's pile and choose a palm branch. Have the child read the action on the front of the branch. You may need to help younger children read.

- The child must hold onto the palm branch and do the action (hop, crawl, tiptoe, or jump) while returning back to the team to tag the next child in line.

- When the team is finished, everyone on the team waves the palm branches in the air and shouts, "Hosanna!"

- Make sure the children understand the directions and begin the game.

- **Say:** When Jesus came to Jerusalem, crowds of people came to see him. The people shouted, "Hosanna! Blessed is the one who comes in the name of the Lord!" (Mark 11:9)

- Instruct the children to do their action again as they move to sit down in the large group area. They will need their palm branch cards during "Sound Effects Studio."

Participation Pageant

- **Say:** Everyone will help tell today's Bible story. First I need one volunteer who wants to play the part of Jesus.

- Choose a child to be Jesus. Have the child come to the stage.

- **Say:** Next I need a volunteer to be the donkey.

- Choose a child to be the donkey. Have the child get down on his or her hands and knees in front of Jesus.

- **Say:** When Jesus rides the donkey into town, you will crawl on your hands and knees in front of Jesus.

- Have Jesus and the donkey practice.

- **Say:** Next I need two volunteers to play the disciples.

- Choose two volunteers to be two of Jesus' disciples.

- **Say:** Great! Now the rest of you will be the crowd.

Prepare

✓ Provide: two pieces of wood

✓ Photocopy and cut out the palm branch cards on page 12. Make enough copies so that each child will have a palm branch.

- Divide the group into two sections. Have the children move so there is a middle aisle between the groups.

- **Say:** I want this group over here *(point to one side of the room)* to stand up, pretend to wave your palm branches, and shout "Hosanna!" I want this group over here *(point to the other side of the room)* to stand up and pretend to lay a cloak on the ground. Let's practice.

- Point to each group and encourage them to do the motions.

- **Say:** As the story begins, the donkey is over here. *(Have the donkey move to one side of the stage.)* And Jesus is talking to his friends over here. *(Have Jesus and his friends move to the other side of the stage.)*

- Tell the story "Hosanna! Hosanna!" on page 12.

The Reason for the Donkey

- Have Jesus and the donkey move across the front of your large group area one more time.

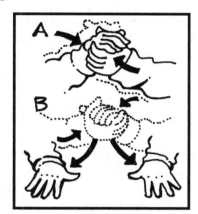

Peace

- **Say:** It is important to know that Jesus rode into Jerusalem on a donkey. Usually a king or other special person would ride into a city on a horse. When Jesus rode into the city on the donkey, he was showing people that he came in peace.

- Teach the children the word *peace* in American Sign Language.

- **Peace:** Place the right palm on top of the left palm. Turn the hands so that the left palm is on top of the right palm. Move both hands down and to the sides.

Sound Effects Studio

- **Say:** Let's remember both the palm branches and the donkey as we say today's Bible verse.

- **Say the Bible verse for the children:** "Hosanna! Blessed is the one who comes in the name of the Lord!" (Mark 11:9).

- Give each child a palm branch card.

- Divide the children into two groups.

- **Say:** Let's say the Bible verse together. When I point to group one, everyone wave your palm branch cards in the air and shout, "Hosanna!" When I point to group two, everyone slap their hands on the floor to make the sound of donkey hooves. While you are slapping your hands say, "Blessed is the one who comes in the name of the Lord!"

- Say the Bible verse several times, switching the groups.

Prepare
✓ Reuse the cards you photocopied for "Palm Promenade" on page 8.

Small Groups

Divide the children into small groups. You may organize the groups around age levels or around readers and nonreaders. Keep the groups small, with a maximum of ten children in each group. You may need to have more than one of each group.

- Give each child a piece of green construction paper and a crayon or colored pencil.

- Encourage the children to work together to trace around each other's hands to make handprints.

- Instruct each child to cut out his or her handprint using safety scissors.

- **Say:** Today our Bible story was about the time Jesus rode a donkey into Jerusalem.

- **Ask:** What did the people do when they saw Jesus coming into the city? *(They waved palm branches and laid branches and coats on the ground for the donkey to walk on.)* Why is it important that Jesus rode a donkey instead of a horse? *(It showed that Jesus came in peace.)*

- **Ask:** What are some ways that we can show peace? *(Be kind to one another, say "please" and "thank you," use our words instead of hitting when we are angry or frustrated, share our toys and art supplies, be helpful, and so forth.)*

- **Say:** Write one thing on your handprint that you can do this week to show peace. It might be one of the things we talked about, or it might be something that you can do for your family—like play with your younger brother so that your mother or father may rest for a few minutes.

- Have the children write on their handprints. Help those who need help.

- **Say:** Now let's turn our handprints into palm branches.

- Glue the strip of green construction paper in the middle of a large piece of mural paper. The strip will become the center stem of the palm branch.

- Place the mural paper on the floor, or tape it on a wall at a height that the children can reach.

- Have (or help) each child read her or his statement to the class and then glue the handprint on either side of the construction paper strip. The handprints will make the leaves of the palm branch.

- Invite the group to stand around or in front of the finished palm branch.

- **Say the Bible verse together:** "Hosanna! Blessed is the one who comes in the name of the Lord!" (Mark 11:9).

- **Pray:** Thank you, God, for Jesus. Help us show peace to everyone we meet. Amen.

Prepare

✓ Provide: green construction paper, crayons or colored pencils, safety scissors, glue, mural paper, masking tape

✓ Cut a 2-inch wide strip from green construction paper. The strip needs to be long enough to allow each child to add his or her handprint on either side of the strip.

Large-Group Worship

Bring everyone together for a time of closing worship.

- Have the children bring the handprint palm branch mural to your worship area. Place the banner over a table, or tape it to a wall.

- Encourage the children to sit down in your worship area.

- Teach the children to sing the song "See Jesus Riding By." The song is sung to the tune of "Down by the Riverside."

We're gonna wave all our branches high.
(Pretend to wave palm branches.)
See Jesus riding by,
See Jesus riding by,
See Jesus riding by.
We're gonna wave all our branches high.
(Pretend to wave palm branches.)
See Jesus riding by,
See Jesus riding by.

We're gonna shout "Hosanna to our king!"
(Cup hands around mouth.)
See Jesus riding by,
See Jesus riding by,
See Jesus riding by.

We're gonna shout "Hosanna to our king!"
(Cup hands around mouth.)
See Jesus riding by,
See Jesus riding by.

We're gonna clap our hands and stomp our feet!
(Clap hands; stomp feet.)
See Jesus riding by,
See Jesus riding by,
See Jesus riding by.
We're gonna clap our hands and stomp our feet!
(Clap hands; stomp feet.)
See Jesus riding by,
See Jesus riding by,

Words: Daphna Flegal
© 2001 Abingdon Press

- Choose a child to bring the open Bible to the front of the room. Have the child place the Bible on the altar, or stand with the Bible while the Bible verse is said.

- **Say the Bible verse together with the children:** "Hosanna! Blessed is the one who comes in the name of the Lord!" (Mark 11:9).

- Choose one or more children to bring the palm crosses to the altar or to the front of the room.

- **Say:** We will give these crosses to the people who come to church (or to the study). The crosses can help us remember Jesus and today's Bible story. Let's bless these crosses.

- **Pray:** God, we praise you for Jesus. Bless the people who made these crosses, and bless the people who will receive these crosses. Help us remember that when Jesus rode into the city of Jerusalem, he came in peace. Amen.

- Sign the word *peace* with the children (see page 9).

- Let the children distribute the crosses, or save them for next week.

✓ Provide the handprint palm branch mural that was made during small group time.

✓ Provide palm crosses made earlier in the lesson.

✓ Provide: a Bible, tape

Hosanna! Hosanna!

by Daphna Flegal

(Jesus and the disciples are on one side of the stage. The donkey is on the other side of the stage.)

One day Jesus and his friends were going to Jerusalem. Just before they got to the city, Jesus stopped.

(Jesus and the disciples walk in place; then stop.)

"Go into the village over there. You will find a donkey tied up. Untie it and bring it here."

(Two disciples go to the donkey. The donkey follows them and stops in front of Jesus.)

Two of Jesus' friends found the donkey and brought it to Jesus.

Jesus sat on the donkey. He began riding into Jerusalem.

(The child playing the donkey crawls on his or her hands and knees in front of the child playing Jesus as

Jesus walks across the stage or down the center aisle between audience groups.)

When the people saw Jesus riding on the donkey, they began to shout, "Hosanna!"

As they shouted, some of the people waved palm branches high in the air.

(Have one side of the audience stand up and pretend to wave palm branches in the air.)

Other people took off their cloaks and placed them on the ground in front of the donkey.

(Have the other side of the audience stand up and pretend to place their cloaks on the ground.)

The people were excited to see Jesus riding on the donkey.

"Hosanna! Hosanna!" everyone shouted. "Blessed is the one who comes in the name of the Lord! Hosanna in the highest!"

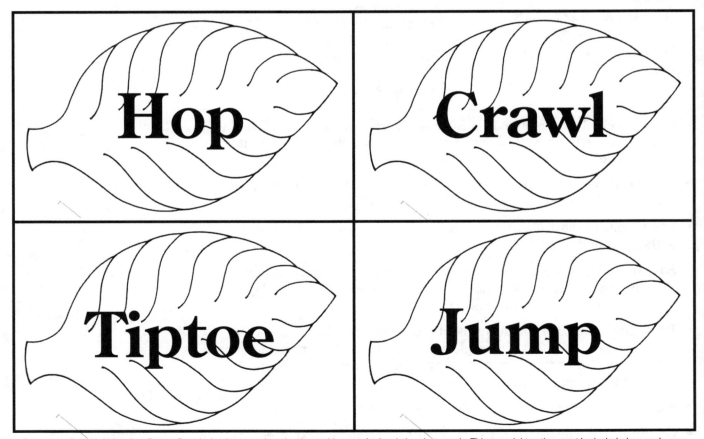

Dear Parents,

Your children are learning about "Bless My Sole,"
a special ministry hosted by Centenary United
Methodist Church in Richmond, Virginia. Every Friday
at "Bless My Sole" volunteers wash the feet of "their
friends on the street," also providing them with a
good meal and meeting any other needs they might
have.

Help your church support "Bless My Sole" by having
your child bring in socks (good quality white cotton;
men's and women's sizes) that the ministry needs to
take care of its city's residents who are without a
home.

Bring your items to your child's class by

_____,2011

2 JESUS WASHES DISCIPLES' FEET

Objectives

The children will
- hear John 13:1-15;
- discover that Jesus became like a servant and washed his friends' feet;
- understand that Jesus wanted his friends to serve others;
- begin a service project.

Bible Story

John 13:1-15: Jesus washes the disciples' feet.

Bible Verse

John 13:15, CEV: I have set the example, and you should do for each other exactly what I have done for you.

Focus for the Teacher

What Does It Mean?

Jesus and his friends came to Jerusalem to celebrate the Passover. The people greeted them with great "Hosannas." But now preparations had to be made to celebrate the traditional Passover meal.

In the Gospel of John, Jesus dramatically rose from the table and took a towel and a basin of water, washing his disciples' feet. No servant had been provided for this task. Jesus himself washed their feet in this instance, since none of the disciples left their places to see to this duty.

Foot washing was a question of hygiene in the first century. The visitor washed his own feet. Or the host would, as an act of hospitality, provide a servant to wash the visitor's feet.

Peter protested Jesus' action at first, believing the action was too degrading a task for Jesus. It was a task that the disciples should have done for Jesus. But Jesus showed his friends that they should be willing to serve one another, just as he served them.

There was also another level to this conversation. Jesus used the foot washing as a metaphor for the degrading death that he was about to face. The disciples could have no part of Jesus unless he died for them.

> I have set the example, and you should do for each other exactly what I have done for you.
> John 13:15, CEV

The Bible Verse

Jesus' washing of the disciples' feet is a startling example of servanthood, a humbling duty reserved for only the lowliest. It was a new way of looking at life for the disciples.

Serving Opportunities

Today servanthood is still part of being a disciple. Your children will have the opportunity to practice servanthood with the "Bless My Sole" program at Centenary United Methodist Church in Richmond, Virginia.

Children enjoy helping others. They are usually the first to volunteer for a task to assist an adult, as long as this does not involve cleaning their rooms. All they need is to be given the opportunity. Jesus was an excellent teacher. He taught by example. Not only did he tell his friends that they had to be servants, but also he showed them how it was done. Set the example for your children during this lesson as well as during the lessons to come.

Explore Interest Groups

Be sure that adult leaders are waiting when the first child arrives. Greet and welcome each child. Get the child involved in an activity that interests him or her and introduces the theme for the day's activities.

Continue Palm Leaf Crosses (if needed)

- If more palm leaf crosses are needed, have the children follow the directions on page 5 to make them.

- Set them aside in a safe place until enough crosses are made for the congregation.

Stamp a Towel

- Cover the table with newspapers and have the children wear paint smocks.

- Show the children the towel and bowl.

- **Say:** Today our Bible story is about the time Jesus shared a special meal with his friends. The meal was part of Passover, an important celebration for the Hebrew people. During the meal Jesus got up from the table and took a towel *(show the children the towel)*. Then he poured water into a bowl *(show the children the bowl)*. He used the water and bowl to wash his friends' dirty feet.

- **Say:** In Bible times people often went barefoot or wore sandals. They walked over rocky, dirty, and dusty roads.

- **Ask:** What do you think happened to a person's feet in Bible times? *(They got dirty.)*

- **Say:** When Bible-times people went to someone's house, usually a servant would wash the guests' feet as they came in. But in our Bible story no one acted as the servant, so no one's feet were washed when they entered the house.

- **Ask:** Do you think it surprised everyone when Jesus acted as the servant and washed his friends' feet? How do you think his friends felt? What do you think Jesus was trying to show his friends? *(That everyone must be willing to serve others.)*

- **Say:** Let's put footprints onto these towels to remind us that we can serve others. First we'll make footprint stamps.

- Give each child a piece of craft foam.

- Have the children help each other trace their footprints onto the foam.

- Have the children use safety scissors to cut out the footprints.

- Let the children glue their footprints to a piece of cardboard.

- Make a paint pad by folding paper towels and placing them into the bottom of a shallow tray. Pour tempera paint onto the paper towels.

Prepare

- ✓ Photocopy the instructions (page 5) for each child.

- ✓ Provide: fresh, moist palm fronds, scissors

- ✓ Cut palm fronds into 14-inch lengths. You will need two strips per cross.

Prepare

- ✓ Provide: a towel and bowl, newspapers, smocks, craft foam, pencils, safety scissors, glue, pieces of cardboard (about the size of a child's foot), toweling or muslin, shallow trays, paper towels, tempera paint, masking tape, pen

- ✓ Cut toweling or muslin into pieces, twelve to eighteen inches long. You will need one for each child.

- Give each child a cloth towel. Instruct the child to spread the towel flat on the work surface.

- Show each child how to hold the stamp by the cardboard and press the foam footprint onto the paint pad and then onto the towel to make prints.

- Place the towels flat to dry. Write the child's name on a piece of masking tape and tape it to the towel. Plan to use the towels in closing worship.

Toeriffic Art

- Spread the mural paper on the floor. Place chairs around the edge of the paper.

- Have the children sit down in the chairs. Encourage the children to take off their shoes and socks and place them under their chairs.

- Give each child two pieces of masking tape and two crayons. Instruct the children to wrap the tape around the middle of the crayons.

- Show the children how to place the crayons between their big toes and second toes.

- Encourage the children to draw on the mural paper.

- **Say:** Bare feet are an important part of today's Bible story. In Bible times people often went barefoot or wore sandals. Their feet got dirty. When Bible-times people went to someone's house, usually a servant would wash the guests' feet as they came in. But in our Bible story Jesus acted as the servant and washed his friends' feet.

- Plan to use the decorated paper as a tablecloth for "Prepare the Table."

Prepare
✓ Provide: mural paper, crayons, masking tape, scissors
✓ Cut the mural paper to fit as a tablecloth for the "Prepare the Table" activity on page 17.

A Quick Wash

- Have the children move to an open area of the room.

- Divide the children into teams. Have the teams line up on one side of the room.

- Place a trash can at the beginning of each line.

- On the opposite side of the room, place an empty bowl and a bowl partially filled with water on a plastic tablecloth or on a towel. Place a stack of paper cups and a stack of paper towels beside each bowl.

- **Say:** In Bible times people washed their hands before they ate. The host or servant would hold the bowl under the guests' hands. Then the host or servant would pour water over the guests' hands. The bowl would catch the water.

- Ask a child or teacher to help you demonstrate the hand washing.

- Have the first two people from each team run to the team's bowls. The first child should hold his or her hands over the empty bowl. The second child should use a paper cup to dip water from the first bowl and pour it over the first child's hand. Then have the children switch. After each child has washed his or her hands, they are to dry their hands with paper towels.

Prepare
✓ Provide for each team: two unbreakable bowls, water, paper cups, paper towels, plastic tablecloth or towel, trash can

- Then have the two children run back to their team, throw the paper towels in the trash can, and tag the next two children in line.

- When the team is finished, everyone on the team sits down and folds their clean hands in their laps.

- Make sure the children understand the directions, then begin the game.

- **Say:** Today our Bible story is about the time Jesus shared a special meal with his friends. During the meal Jesus got up from the table and took a towel. Then he poured water into a bowl. He used the water and bowl to wash his friends' feet.

Prepare the Table

- **Say:** In Bible times people ate around tables that were about the height of today's coffee table. The table usually had three sides, like a U-shape. The table was surrounded by couches or pillows. People reclined on the couches by leaning on their left side. Their feet would have been stretched out away from the table.

- Encourage the children to help you set up a table like in Bible times.

- Use a coffee table or fold up the legs of a folding table and set the table on the floor.

- Cover the table with the "Toeriffic Art" mural paper.

- Have the children place pillows around the table.

Prepare
✓ Provide: a coffee table or folding table, pillows, Toeriffic mural made earlier

Passover Food Tasting

- Make sure the children have washed their hands before experiencing this activity.

- Have the children sit down on the floor or around the table they helped set up earlier. Encourage the children to lean onto their left elbow and stretch their legs out away from the table.

- Say a blessing with the children.

- Give each child a piece of pita bread.

- Show the children the haroseth (huh-ROSE-uth) you prepared ahead.

- Let each child sample the haroseth by dipping a piece of pita bread into the haroseth bowl. Do <u>not</u> allow double dipping!

- **Say:** Today our Bible story is about the time Jesus shared a special meal with his friends. The meal was part of Passover, an important celebration for the Hebrew people. During Passover the people remember how they escaped from slavery in Egypt.

- **Say:** You are tasting haroseth, one of the foods served at the Passover meal. The haroseth reminded the people of the mortar that the slaves used to build the pyramids. Jesus and his friends would have had haroseth at their Passover meal.

Prepare
✓ Provide: hand-washing supplies, pita bread, serving bowl, haroseth

✓ <u>Prepare haroseth ahead:</u>
3 apples peeled; chopped
⅛ cup chopped almonds
½ T. sugar
¼ tsp. cinnamon
grated lemon rind
2 T. grape juice

Mix together in a large bowl.

Large Group

Bring all the children together to experience the Bible story. Tap a spoon on the side of a metal bowl or pan to alert the children to the large group time. Use the transition activity to move the children from the interest groups to the large group area.

Bowl and Towel Tag

- Give each child a bowl/towel square.

- Have the children fold the squares along the dotted line.

- **Say:** Today our Bible story is about the time when Jesus shared a special meal with his friends. During the meal Jesus got up from the table and took a towel *(show the children the towel picture on the square)*. Then he poured water into a bowl *(show the children the bowl picture on the square)*. He used the water and bowl to wash his friends' feet.

- Have the children stand in a line. Count off 1, 2, 1, 2, 1, 2, and so forth.

- **Say:** All the one's are the towel. All the two's are the bowl.

- Have all the one's tape their squares to their clothing so that the towel picture is showing. Have all the two's tape their squares to their clothing so that the bowl picture is showing.

- **Say:** When I say "towels!", all the towels will try to tag the bowls. When a bowl is tagged, he or she turns over the square and becomes a towel. You may need to retape your square. When I say "bowls," all the bowls will try to tag the towels.

- Switch the names frequently enough to keep the children moving and constantly changing from towel to bowl.

- End the game by having all the towels sit down in the large group area. Then have all the bowls sit down.

Footlight Theater Presents

- Prepare two foot puppets for the presentation.

- Trace an adult-size foot onto posterboard (you will need two), or use the footprint on page 22 as a pattern. Cut the footprints out.

- Decorate the two footprints with faces. One footprint will represent Peter, and the other, John.

- Glue or tape the footprints onto dowel rods or yardsticks.

- Set up a puppet stage in the front of your large group area.

- Present the puppet play "Clean Feet" using the foot puppets.

- **Note:** You may make the puppets larger by enlarging the original footprint on a copy machine.

Prepare

✓ Provide: a spoon and a metal bowl or pan

✓ Photocopy the towel and bowl squares on page 22. Each child will need a copy.

✓ Provide: masking tape

Prepare

✓ Recruit two older children, youth, or adults to be the puppeteers.

✓ Photocopy the script (page 23) for the puppeteers.

✓ Photocopy the footprint pattern (page 22).

✓ Provide: posterboard, adult scissors, markers, glue, tape, and dowel rods or yardsticks

✓ Provide: paints, fabric scraps, yarn, and glue to decorate the puppets

✓ Set up a puppet stage in your large group area. It may be a table turned on its side, a piece of mural paper or fabric held up by two volunteers, or a sheet hung over a row of chairs.

24 Hours That Changed the World (For Younger Children)

An Example to Follow

- **Say:** When Bible-times people went to someone's house, usually a servant would wash the guests' feet as they came in.

- **Ask:** Who washed the guests' feet in today's Bible story? *(Jesus)* Do you think that washing his friends' feet was too icky a task for Jesus? How do you think Jesus felt while he was washing feet? How do you think Jesus' friends felt? What did Jesus tell his friends to do? *(follow his example)*

- **Say:** Jesus showed his friends that they should be willing to serve one another, just as he served them.

- Teach the children the word *serve* in American Sign Language.

- **Serve:** Hold both hands about chest level with palms facing up. Move each hand back and forth alternately.

Serve

Bible Verse Repeat

- **Say:** Our Bible verse today is John 13:15, CEV: "I have set the example, and you should do for each other exactly what I have done for you."

- Have the children repeat the Bible verse.

- **Say:** When I said the Bible verse before you repeated it, I gave you an example of how to say the Bible verse. I'm going to give you more examples of ways you can say this Bible verse. I want you to repeat the verse just like I say in the example. Let's begin by standing.

- Have the children stand up.

- **Say:** I *(point to yourself)* have set *(sit down)* the example.

- Have the children repeat the verse, point to themselves, and sit down.

- **Say:** and you *(point to another person)* should do for each other…

- Have the children repeat the verse and point to each other.

- **Say:** exactly what I *(point to yourself)* have done for you *(point to another person)*.

- Have the children repeat the verse and point to themselves and each other.

- Repeat the verse again, using the same motions and changing the volume in your voice.

- Have the children stand up.

- **Say:** *(softly)* I have set *(sit down)* the example, and *(loudly)* you *(point to another person)* *(softly)* should do for *(loudly)* each other exactly what *(softly)* I *(point to yourself)* have done for *(loudly)* you *(point to another person)*.

Small Groups

Divide the children into small groups. You may organize the groups around age levels or around readers and nonreaders. Keep the groups small, with a maximum of ten children in each group. You may need to have more than one of each group.

- Give each child the "Bless My Sole" note.

- **Say:** Every week, a few people from Centenary United Methodist Church in Richmond, Virginia, wash the feet of those in need who come to the church for a meal. They also give people a clean pair of socks to wear. The program is called "Bless My Sole." This note tells about the program and invites you to help by bringing a pair of clean socks. After we collect the socks, we will send them to Centenary United Methodist for "Bless My Sole."

- Encourage the children to decorate the notes by making pretend footprints.

- Fold paper towels and place them in the bottom of shallow trays. Pour tempera paint over the paper towels to make paint pads.

- Show the children how to make footprints using the side of one hand.

- First have the children curl one of their hands into a fist.

- Next have the children press the side of their fists onto a paint pad, then onto their notes. This will make the bottom of the footprint.

- Next, have the children press a thumb onto a paint pad. Then have the children make a thumbprint in the big toe spot above the footprint.

- Encourage the children to use their fingers to make fingerprints for the remaining toes.

- Let the children make several footprints on their notes.

- Set the notes aside to dry.

- When the children are finished, have them clasp their hands together to keep the paint from dripping or spreading to other areas.

- Place a bowl of water and some soap on the table, and have towels nearby.

- **Say:** In our Bible story today Jesus acted as a servant and washed his friends' feet. Right now your hands need washing. Let me wash your hands.

- Go to each child and wash the paint off her or his hands. Dry the child's hands with a towel.

- **Say the Bible verse for each child:** "I have set the example, and you should do for each other exactly what I have done for you" (John 13:15, CEV) as you are washing his or her hands.

Prepare

- ✓ Photocopy the note about "Bless My Sole" (page 13) for each child.

- ✓ Provide: paint smocks, paper towels, tempera paints, shallow trays, bowl, water, soap, towels

- To learn more about "Bless My Sole" go to, http://www.centumc.org/blessmysole.htm.

- If you have Internet access together, watch the YouTube video at http://www.youtube.com/watch?v=msaU6yR3bA4.

NOTE: *Websites are constantly changing. Although these websites were checked at the time this book was edited, we recommend that you double check the site to verify that it is still live and that it is still appropriate for children before doing the activity.*

Large-Group Worship

Bring everyone together for a time of closing worship.

- Encourage the children to sit down in your worship area.

- Teach the children to sing the song "Dirty Feet." The song is sung to the tune of "Hot Cross Buns."

  Dirty feet *(eww!)*
  Dirty feet *(eww!)*
  Jesus' friends came to the meal with
  Dirty feet *(eww!)*

  Wash their feet *(ah!)*
  Wash their feet *(ah!)*
  Jesus got up from the meal to
  Wash their feet *(ah!)*

  Washing feet *(oh!)*
  Washing feet *(oh!)*
  Jesus showed us how to serve by
  Washing feet *(oh!)*

- Choose a child to bring the open Bible to the front of the room. Have the child place the Bible on the altar, or stand while the Bible verse is said.

- **Say the Bible verse together:** "I have set the example, and you should do for each other exactly what I have done for you" (John 13:15, CEV).

- Sign the word *serve* with the children (see page 19).

- Have the stamped towels the children made earlier within reach.

- Call each child up by name.

- **Say:** (Child's name), Jesus set an example for you. Remember to serve others.

- Then give the child his or her towel.

- Continue until you have called every child and presented her or him with a towel.

- If you have not given out the palm crosses, choose a child to bring the crosses to your worship area.

- **Say:** We will give these crosses to the people who come to church (or to the study). The crosses can help us remember Jesus and today's Bible story. Let's bless these crosses.

- **Pray:** God, we praise you for Jesus. Bless the people who made these crosses and bless the people who will receive these crosses. Help us remember that Jesus taught us to serve one another. Amen.

- Let the children distribute the crosses.

Prepare

✓ Provide the stamped towels made earlier in the lesson.

✓ Optional: Provide palm crosses made earlier in the lesson.

✓ Provide: a Bible

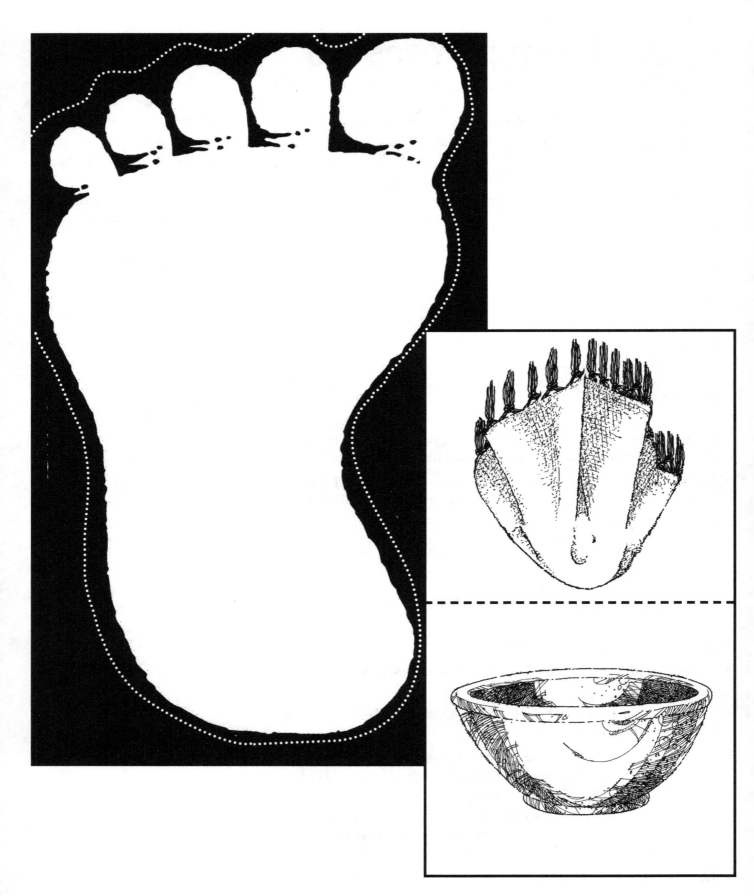

24 Hours That Changed the World (For Younger Children)

Clean Feet

by Daphna Flegal

Peter's Foot: I'm Peter's foot. I've been helping him walk all his life.

John's Foot: And I'm John's foot. Lately we've been following a man named Jesus.

Peter's Foot: And doing a lot of walking!

John's Foot: We really have walked a lot this week. First, Jesus decided it was time to go to Jerusalem. He sent a couple of us to walk to a nearby village for a donkey.

Peter's Foot: When we brought him the donkey, we laid our cloaks over its back so Jesus could sit on it. Then Jesus rode the donkey into the city. Of course, we walked!

John's Foot: But it was exciting. We walked beside Jesus, looking and listening as crowds of people shouted, "Hosanna!"

Peter's Foot: Today it's time to celebrate the Passover meal. Jesus sent Peter and me to get the meal ready.

John's Foot: When Peter had everything ready, we all walked to the house for the celebration.

Peter's Foot: Usually when we enter a house, a servant greets us and washes us.

John's Foot: It feels great! The roads are dirty and dusty. My toes really start to sweat.

Peter's Foot: And smell!

John's Foot: Well, yes, but your toes smell too!

Peter's Foot: They can't help it. You know we walk everywhere we go and our sandals don't keep out the dirt.

John's Foot: Which is why it feels so good to be washed.

Peter's Foot: It really does. But there was no washing today. So we all just sat around the table smelly and dirty.

John's Foot: Everyone was eating together when Jesus did something surprising.

Peter's Foot: He stood up, took off his cloak, and tied a towel around his waist.

John's Foot: Then he poured water into a bowl and began to wash us — just like he was our servant instead of our teacher.

Peter's Foot: Peter was upset. I was too. No, Jesus! Don't wash me!

John's Foot: "Unless I wash you," Jesus said to Peter, "then you don't really belong to me."

Peter's Foot: "Then wash my hands and my head as well," said Peter. I agreed.

John's Foot: After Jesus washed all of us, he put his cloak back on and sat back down.

Peter's Foot: "Do you understand what I just did?" Jesus asked everyone at the table. "I am your teacher, but I don't think I am so much better than you that I can't wash the dirt from your feet."

John's Foot: Then Jesus said, "I have set the example, and you should do for each other exactly what I have done for you."

Peter's Foot: I don't think I understand, but it does feel good to be clean.

3 THE LAST SUPPER

Objectives

The children will
- hear Luke 22:7-34;
- learn that Jesus gave his disciples a new way to remember him;
- realize that we remember Jesus when we celebrate Communion;
- continue the service project.

Bible Story

Luke 22:7-34: The Last Supper

Bible Verse

Luke 22:19, GNT: Do this in memory of me.

Focus for the Teacher

Passover

Passover is a Jewish religious festival that celebrates God's deliverance of the Hebrew people from slavery in Egypt. Originally, persons could observe Passover at home or in the local shrines. But King Josiah after the return from Exile decreed Passover as a pilgrimage feast. Persons who were able had to go to the Temple in Jerusalem and make their sacrifice of the paschal lamb. During Passover Jerusalem's population swelled by hundreds of thousands of pilgrims.

> Do this in memory of me.
> Luke 22:19, GNT

For an entire week the people ate unleavened bread to remind them of the Hebrew's quick departure from Egypt. During a commemorative meal they ate lamb, along with bitter herbs and wine. The blood of the lamb was a reminder of God's covenant with the people of Israel.

The number of pilgrims surpassed the places available to celebrate the Passover. People with extra rooms rented or loaned them to travelers to use for their celebrations. Jesus and his friends came to eat the commemorative meal together in such a room.

Jesus and his followers formed a family unit. As such, they came to celebrate the feast days together. During the Passover meal Jesus sat at the table with his twelve apostles. He served as head of the family group, saying the special blessings designated to the father.

But on this particular night Jesus had another message to deliver. Near the end of the meal he broke a bit of the bread and invited his disciples to share it.

Then he took the familiar cup of wine and asked them to drink from it. Through his actions he told them not only what was about to happen to him, but also that he would always be present with them.

The Bible Verse

Through the Passover meal, known today as the Last Supper, Jesus gave his disciples a new way to remember him.

Holy Communion

Many younger elementary children have participated in Holy Communion. They have heard the words and have taken the bread and juice. But remember, they are concrete thinkers. The idea of Jesus' body and blood being "given for you and for many" is an abstract concept that may be beyond their level of comprehension. For them it is more important to use the celebration of Communion as a time of remembering Jesus and remembering all that Jesus taught. Invite the pastor to spend time with the children. Explain the various steps of the Communion service. Help the children know what is expected of them.

Explore Interest Groups

Be sure that adult leaders are waiting when the first child arrives. Greet and welcome each child. Get the child involved in an activity that interests him or her and introduces the theme for the day's activities.

Socks Box

- Cover a box with plain paper.

- Encourage the children to decorate the box by gluing on unmatched socks.

- Or let the children use safety scissors to cut sock shapes out of construction paper. Have the children decorate the socks with crayons or markers, then glue the paper socks onto the box.

- **Say:** Let's put the socks we bring for "Bless My Sole" inside this box. In a few weeks we will mail all the socks we have donated to Centenary United Methodist Church in Virginia.

- Thank any child who brought socks and place the socks in the box. Remind the children that they can still bring socks next week.

Prepare

✓ Provide: large box, plain paper, glue, tape, unmatched socks or construction paper for cutting out sock shapes, crayons or markers, safety scissors

Bake Bread

- Cover the table with a plastic tablecloth.

- Have the children wash their hands.

- **Say:** Today our Bible story is about the time when Jesus shared a special meal with his friends. The meal was part of Passover, an important celebration for the Hebrew people. Part of the meal included unleavened bread. *Unleavened* meant that there was no yeast in the bread to make it rise. The bread was flat. Eating the bread helped the Hebrew people remember how Moses led the people out of Egypt. The people had to leave Egypt in such a hurry that the bread did not have time to rise. Let's make unleavened bread.

- Have the children take turns pouring four cups of wheat flour into a large mixing bowl.

- Add a teaspoon of salt and mix together.

- Slowly add one and one-half cups water to the flour and salt until the mixture begins to make a ball.

- Add more water if the dough is too crumbly. Add more flour if the dough is too sticky.

- Place a sheet of wax paper in front of each child to make a work surface.

- Have the children spread a small amount of flour onto the work surface.

- Give each child a portion of the dough. Show the children how to knead the dough. The dough should be kneaded about 10 minutes.

Prepare

✓ Provide: plastic tablecloth, hand-washing supplies, wax paper, wheat flour, salt, water, large mixing bowl, measuring cups and spoons, mixing spoon, potholders, cookie sheets.

- Have the children shape the dough into circles about the size of a small paper plate.
- Place each circle on an ungreased cookie sheet and bake in a preheated 500 degree oven for 5 minutes or until discs are lightly colored, blistered, and crisp. Makes about 16 discs.
- Plan to eat the discs during small group time.

Make Grape Juice

Prepare
✓ Provide: red grapes, large bowl, colander, rotary food press, wooden pestle, small paper cups, hand-washing supplies, paper towels

- Have the children wash their hands.
- **Say:** Wine is made from grapes. In Bible times grapes were harvested and then placed in a wine press. The wine press was a trough or shallow pit lined with stone. Below were bins for catching the juice. The grapes were crushed by rolling a rock around the press, or by people walking on them. The juice ran out through the bottom of the press into bins. People drank the juice or made it into wine.
- Let the children pick the grapes off the stems and discard any grapes that are spoiled.
- Instruct the children to place the grapes in a colander. Place the colander in the sink and wash the grapes by running cold water over them.
- Next, have the children place the grapes in a rotary food press and place it over a large bowl.
- Show the children how to use the wooden pestle to squeeze the grapes against the sides of the food press.
- Let the children take turns squeezing the grapes.
- **Say:** It takes 10 to 12 pounds of grapes to make one gallon of juice.
- **Ask:** What color are the grapes? (red) What color is the juice? (very light) Are you surprised? Did you think it would be red?
- **Say:** When you see red wine or dark-colored grape juice it is because the skins of the grapes were soaked with the juice. The skins are removed, but the darker color stays.
- Pour the juice into cups and let the children taste the juice.
- **Say:** Today our Bible story is about the Passover meal Jesus ate with his friends. Jesus and his friends drank wine and ate bread at the meal. Then Jesus told his friends to remember him each time they ate bread and drank wine together.

Prepare
✓ Photocopy a bread pattern for each child (page 32).

✓ Provide: two clear plastic plates for each child, pencils, safety scissors, black construction paper, different colors of tissue paper, plastic or paper containers, white glue, water, glue brushes

✓ Pour white glue (or glue that will dry clear) into a plastic or paper container. Thin the glue with a small amount of water.

Make Stained-glass Bread Plates

- **Say:** After Jesus shared the Passover meal with his friends, he took a loaf of bread and gave thanks for it. Then he broke the bread and gave it to his friends. He told his friends to remember him each time they ate bread together. Today when we eat bread and drink juice at Holy Communion, we remember Jesus. Let's make bread plates that we can use at Communion.

- Have the children use safety scissors to cut out the bread patterns.

- Have the children trace the bread patterns onto black construction paper and then cut them out to make bread silhouettes.

- Give each child two clear plastic plates.

- Have each child turn over one of the plastic plates. Then have the child brush water-thinned glue all over the back of the plate.

- Let each child press the bread silhouette onto the center back of the plate.

- Have the children tear or cut colored tissue paper into small pieces.

- Let the children press the tissue paper over the glue on the back of the plate to create a stained-glass look.

- Encourage the children to cover the entire back. The children may need to brush on more glue.

- Have the children brush another layer of glue over the tissue paper.

- Then have each child place the second clear plate onto the decorated plate so that the silhouette and tissue paper are sandwiched between the plates.

- Set the plates aside to dry. Plan to use the plates in your small groups.

Find the Chametz

- Hide croutons around the room before the children gather for the game.

- **Say:** Jesus and his friends celebrated the Passover meal because they were good and faithful Jews. Jewish people all over the world still celebrate Passover.

  Jewish children play a game called *chametz* (chah-maytyz) to prepare for Passover. They search all over the house and find any bread that has been made with leavening (the yeast that makes the bread rise). They must collect the bread to throw away because there cannot be any leavened bread in the house.

  Let's search for bread in this room. We will use the bread we find to feed the birds.

- Give each child a feather.

- Encourage the children to search around the room to find the hidden croutons. Anyone who finds a crouton calls an adult, who comes with a bowl. The child sweeps the bread into the bowl with the feather.

- Declare a celebration when all the bread is found.

- Take the croutons outside to feed the birds or plan to do this task later.

adapted from PowerXpress! The Lord's Supper © 2003 Abingdon Press

Prepare
✓ Provide: bowl, croutons, a feather for each child

Large Group

Bring all the children together to experience the Bible story. Tap a spoon on the side of a metal bowl or pan to alert the children to the large group time. Use the transition activity to move the children from the interest groups to the large group area.

Memory Game

- Stand in one corner of the room and hold a tray of items.
- **Say:** Before you sit down in our large group area, each of you must come by me and look at the items on my tray.
- Have each child walk by you, look at the tray, and then sit down.
- Put the tray on the stage area and cover it with a cloth or towel.
- **Say:** Now let's test your memories.
- Mount a large piece of paper on a wall or easel in your stage area.
- **Say:** Call out all the items you remember seeing on the tray.
- Write each item on the paper as the children name them.
- Uncover the tray and see if any item was forgotten.
- Take the tray where the children cannot see it and remove one item.
- Bring the tray back in.
- **Say:** Now look at the tray and tell me what item is missing.
- Let the children guess the missing item.
- **Say:** In our Bible story today Jesus gives his friends a special way to remember him. Let's find out what it is.

Footlight Theater Presents

- Prepare four sock puppets for the presentation.
- Use four adult-size white socks. One sock will be Jesus and the other three the disciples. Draw faces on the socks and glue pieces of fabric over the heads of the puppets.
- Present the play "Remember Me" to the children using the sock puppets.

A Sign to Help Your Memory

- **Ask:** What did Jesus want us to do in memory of him? *(eat the bread and drink the juice)* What do we call it at church when we eat bread and drink juice together? *(Holy Communion)* How does eating bread and drinking juice help us remember Jesus?
- **Say:** When we eat bread and drink juice at Holy Communion, it reminds us of the special meal Jesus shared with his friends. It also reminds us that Jesus is with us and loves us.

Prepare

- ✓ Provide: a spoon and a metal bowl or pan
- ✓ Provide: tray, 8 to 10 items for the tray (bread, Communion cups, bread basket, bottle of grape juice, napkins, Bible, bookmark, flower, cross, and so forth), towel or fabric to cover the objects, newsprint or large paper, markers, tape or easel

Prepare

- ✓ Recruit older children, youth, or adults to be the narrator and the four puppets. Designate one puppet to be Jesus.
- ✓ Photocopy the script (pages 32–33) for the actors.
- ✓ Provide adult-size socks, and fabric scraps, yarn, markers, and glue to decorate the puppets.
- ✓ Set up a puppet stage in your large group area. It may be a table turned on its side, a piece of mural paper or fabric held up by two volunteers, or a sheet hung over a row of chairs.

- Teach the children the word *remember* in American Sign Language.
- **Remember:** Curl both hands into fists with the thumbs out. Touch the right thumb to your forehead. Bring your right fist down alongside of your face and then place your right thumb on top of your left thumb.

Bible Verse Litany

- **Say:** Our Bible verse today is "Do this in memory of me" (Luke 22:19, GNT).

- Have the children repeat the Bible verse.

- **Say:** Jesus told his friends to remember him every time they ate bread and drank the cup of wine. When we do certain things, we can remember Jesus too.

- Show the children the bread basket.

- **Say:** This is some of the bread we made earlier today. The bread reminds us of how Jesus shared a special meal with his friends. I will hold the basket and walk around where you are sitting as the music plays. When the music stops, I will give the basket to someone near me. After you take the basket, stand up. Please don't eat the bread. We will be able to eat the bread during our small group time. As you hold the basket, tell us something you remember about Jesus. For example, you might say, "I remember Jesus loves me." After each person's statement, we will all say the Bible verse together.

- Have a helper or another teacher play music on an instrument or from a CD. Walk through where the children are sitting. Have the helper randomly stop the music. Give the basket to one of the children. Have that child stand up and say what he or she remembers about Jesus. Then encourage everyone to say the Bible verse together.

- Continue the activity until several (or all) children have had an opportunity to hold the basket.

Move to Small Groups

- **Say:** It's time to move to our small groups. Before we go, I will call each of you by name. When you hear your name, get up and look for the bread plate you decorated earlier today. If you did not make a bread plate, go and get a clear plate. Bring your bread plate with you to your small group.

- Call the names of two or three children at a time.

- **Say:** (Children's names), "Remember Jesus."

- Continue until you have called all the children.

Prepare

✓ Provide: unleavened bread baked earlier in the lesson, basket, napkin, adult or older child helper, musical instrument or music CD and CD player

✓ Line a basket with a napkin. Place two or three circles of the bread (made earlier today) in the basket.

Prepare

✓ Provide the bread plates made earlier.

Small Groups

Divide the children into small groups. You may organize the groups around age levels or around readers and nonreaders. Keep the groups small, with a maximum of ten children in each group. You may need to have more than one of each group.

- Invite the children to sit down around the table or in a circle on the floor of your small group area.

- Have the children place their stained-glass bread plates in front of them.

- Show the children the cup.

- **Say:** Jesus probably used a cup made of wood or pottery to drink the wine at the Passover meal.

- **Ask:** What did Jesus tell his friends to do with the cup? *(share it with one another)*

- Show the children the plate or basket.

- **Say:** The bread was probably served on a flat basket or a plate made from wood or pottery.

- **Ask:** What did Jesus tell his friends to do with the bread? *(eat it and remember him)*

- **Say:** I will give the cup to the person on my right and say, "This is a cup." The person with the cup asks, "A what?" I will answer, "A cup." The person with the cup passes the cup along and does the same thing. We will continue to do this all around the circle.

- Once you think the children understand the game, start the plate in the opposite direction. At some point the same child will have both the cup and the plate.

  adapted from PowerXpress! The Lord's Supper © 2003 Abingdon Press

- **Say:** The cup and the bread are symbols. When we see the bread and cup during Holy Communion, we remember what Jesus said at the Last Supper. When we eat the bread and drink the juice, we have the opportunity to remember Jesus.

- **Ask:** What do you think about when you are taking Communion? *(Encourage, but do not force, the children to answer.)*

- Show the children the basket of bread.

- Pass the bread basket around the group and encourage each child to take a piece and place it on his or her plate.

- **Pray:** Thank you, Jesus, for giving us the bread as a way to remember your love for us. Amen.

- Let the children eat the bread.

Prepare

- ✓ Provide: a wooden cup (or other unbreakable cup), wooden plate or flat basket, stained-glass bread plates made earlier, unleavened bread discs made earlier, napkins

- ✓ Place a napkin inside a basket. Place the unleavened bread discs made earlier in the basket.

Note: If you wish to serve Communion to your children, check with your pastor.

Large-Group Worship

Bring everyone together for a time of closing worship.

- Teach the children to sing "The Communion Union" to the tune of "Peanut Butter, Jelly."

Join in the Communion Union.
(*All join hands on the word union.*)
Join in the Communion Union.
(*Raise hands in the air.*)

First you take the bread
(*Use your hands and pretend to break a loaf of bread in half.*)
and you break it, you break it,
you break it, break it, break it.

And you eat it, you eat it,
(*Pretend to take bites of bread.*)
you eat it, eat it, eat it.

Join in the Communion Union.
(*All join hands on the word union.*)
Join in the Communion Union.
(*Raise hands in the air.*)

Then you take the cup
(*Pretend to hold a pitcher with one hand and pour contents into a cup in the other hand.*)
and you fill it, you fill it,
you fill it, fill it, fill it.

And you pass it, you pass it,
(*Pretend to pass the cup to someone beside you.*)
you pass it, pass it, pass it.

Join in the Communion Union.
(*All join hands on the word union.*)
Join in the Communion Union.
(*Raise hands in the air.*)

Words: Mark Burrows
© 2002 Abingdon Press

- Choose a child to bring the open Bible to the front of the room. Have the child place the Bible on the altar, or stand with the Bible while the Bible verse is said.

- **Say the Bible verse together with the children:** "Do this in memory of me" (Luke 22:19, GNT).

- Say the following prayer with the children. Have the children say the response, "We remember Jesus." Sign the word *remember* (see page 29) with the children each time the children say the response.

Pray:	**We remember Jesus.**
Jesus had a meal to share.	Jesus' love is with us still.
We remember Jesus.	**We remember Jesus.**
Some of Jesus' friends were there.	Jesus' love is with us still.
We remember Jesus.	**We remember Jesus.**
Bread and juice, they had their fill.	**All:** Amen.

© 2003 Abingdon Press

Prepare
✓ Provide: a Bible

Remind the children that they may still bring socks for "Bless My Sole."

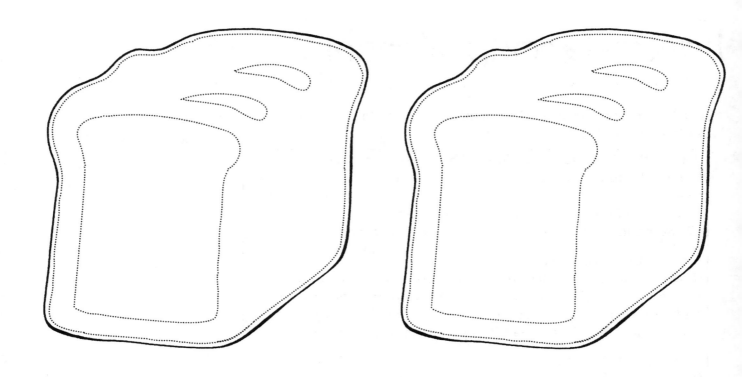

Remember Me

by Daphna Flegal

Narrator: *(whispering)* Good evening. Let me introduce myself. I am the narrator. These are the puppets *(gesture to puppets; puppets bow)*. They are playing the parts of Jesus and his friends.

I, the narrator, will help you understand what is going on in this play. The puppets will help you see what is going on in this play. *(Puppets bow.)*

But I am going to talk very quietly, I don't want to interrupt what is happening. The puppets don't talk at all. *(Puppets bow.)*

Okay, puppets, *(Puppets bow.)* get in your places.

We are about to begin Scene 1. It is the first day of the Feast of the Passover. Jesus and his friends are walking toward Jerusalem, talking together. Puppets, *(Puppets bow.)* start walking.

(Scene 1: A street outside Jerusalem. Puppets walk together back and forth across the stage.)

Narrator: *(whispering)* One of the disciples stops and asks Jesus, "Where shall we go to get ready for the Passover?"

(Puppets keep walking together back and forth across stage.)

Narrator: *(louder)* I said… the disciples stop!

(Puppets abruptly stop walking.)

Narrator: *(whispering)* They ask Jesus, "Where shall we go to get ready for the Passover?"

Jesus told them, "Go into the city. There you will meet a man carrying a water jar. Follow him back to his house. Tell the owner that the Teacher is in need of his guest room to celebrate the Passover. Make preparations for us there."

24 Hours That Changed the World (For Younger Children)

Remember Me

(continued from page 32)

(Puppets walk together back and forth across stage.)

Narrator: *(louder)* A man carrying a water jar?

(Puppets stop and look at narrator.)

Narrator: *(whispering)* Oops, too loud. Sorry. A man carrying a water jar? That shouldn't be hard to find. Usually only women carry water jars. Jesus must have used this like a secret code. And so the disciples easily found the man with the jar. They followed him back to the house.

(Puppets walk together back and forth across stage.)

Narrator: *(whispering)* Now we're ready for Scene 2. It is outside a Bible-times home. A disciple is talking to the man with the water jar. Let's listen.

(Scene 2: Outside a Bible-times home. Three puppets pantomime talking together.)

Narrator: *(whispering)* The disciple says, "The Teacher asks, 'Where is your guest room, where I may eat the Passover with my disciples?'"

Narrator: *(whispering)* The man led the disciples up the stairs on the outside of the house. He was still carrying that water jar. He showed them a large upper room that was already furnished and ready.

(The three puppets pretend to walk up the stairs.)

Narrator: *(whispering)* The disciples began to make preparations for the special evening meal.

(The puppets pretend to walk up the stairs again. They walk for a few minutes.)

Narrator: *(whispering)* Hey! It's only one flight of stairs. You can stop now! *(Puppets stop and bow.)* Soon Jesus and the other disciples arrived and took their places at the table. This is Scene 3. We are inside the upper room. As they ate, Jesus began to speak. Let's listen.

(Scene 3: Inside the upper room. Puppets sit down on floor or around table as if at the Last Supper.)

Narrator: *(whispering)* Jesus held up a loaf of bread and said, "God, we thank you for this bread. Amen. As we eat this bread, think of me. It represents my body."

Then Jesus took the cup of wine and said, "God, we thank you for this cup of wine. Amen. Now drink this, friends. It represents my blood, which will soon be shed for many."

(Puppets turn heads back and forth to look at each other.)

Narrator: *(whispering)* The disciples looked at each other. Body? Blood? What was Jesus saying? The disciples did not know what to do or say. And so they said nothing. After the meal, Jesus went out to the garden to pray… But that's another story.

(Puppets bow and exit.)

adapted from PowerXpress! The Lord's Supper © 2003 Abingdon Press

4 THE GARDEN OF GETHSEMANE

Objectives
The children will
• hear Mark 14:26-42;
• discover that Jesus prayed to God when he was sad and troubled;
• learn that God was with Jesus when Jesus faced troubled times; God is always with us;
• continue the service project.

Bible Story
Mark 14:26-42: Jesus prays.

Bible Verse
Psalm 145:18:
The LORD is near to all who call on him.

Focus for the Teacher

After Dinner

After Jesus and the disciples finished their Passover feast, they sang a hymn and then went to the Mount of Olives.

Before Jesus went into the garden to pray, he told his closest friends, the disciples, that they would desert him in his hour of need. The disciples were upset, and Peter declared that he would never desert Jesus. Jesus told Peter that this very night, before the cock crowed twice, Peter would deny Jesus three times. Peter was upset and denied it. But Jesus knew the disciples well.

Even knowing this, Jesus did not condemn them. If Jesus did not condemn even his closest friends' temporary betrayal, then surely when we are momentarily weak, we will not be condemned.

In the Garden

Jesus went into the garden of Gethsemane to pray. With him he took Peter, James, and John. These three were closest to Jesus and were taken with him when something special was about to occur. (All three were at the Transfiguration.)

The garden may have been an olive grove owned by one of his followers. Obviously it was a place with

> The LORD is near to all who call on him.
> Psalm 145:18

which Jesus was familiar and so, for that matter, was Judas. Judas knew where to take the soldiers so that they could arrest Jesus away from the city and its excitable crowds.

There in the peacefulness of the garden, Jesus asked God for a solution to the problem at hand—a solution that would not mean his having to give his life. Even though Jesus did not happily choose the path that was set before him, he was willing to follow the path because it was God's will.

How hurtful it probably was to discover that his closest friends couldn't stay awake and keep watch with him as he prayed.

Bible Verse

Psalm 145 was written by David and is identified as a psalm of praise. Verse 18 reminds us that if we call on God we will experience God's love and presence.

God Is With Us

God was with Jesus through all of the events of Holy Week. God was always with him, supporting Jesus and helping him face what was going to happen. This will help your children know that bad things do happen, but God is with us.

Explore Interest Groups

Be sure that adult leaders are waiting when the first child arrives. Greet and welcome each child. Get the child involved in an activity that interests him or her and introduces the theme for the day's activities.

Socks Box

- Thank any child who brought socks and place the socks in the box that was decorated last week. Remind the children that they can still bring socks next week.

Discover Olives

- **Say**: In today's Bible story Jesus goes to an olive garden called Gethsemane to pray. Olives grow on trees. The leaves of olive trees are green all year long. The trees are usually short and squat with twisted trunks. Olives were an important food in Bible times.

- Have the children wash their hands.

- Encourage the children to taste the olives you have provided.

- Give each child a paper plate, napkin, spoon, and two crackers. Spoon a bit of plain cream cheese onto each plate.

- Invite the children to spread some cream cheese on their crackers and then select some of the olive pieces to taste on their crackers.

- Encourage them to taste a small piece of the various kinds of olives.

- **Say:** Olives were not only eaten, but also were pressed to make oil. Olives were placed on a circular trough. Then a man or a donkey walked around the circle rolling a stone over the olives. The oil dripped down into a container. Olive oil is still used in cooking today. Sometimes people dip bread into olive oil instead of using butter.

- Give each child a small paper plate, a napkin, and a few pieces of crusty bread. Pour a small amount of extra-virgin olive oil (oil that comes from the first pressing) into a small cup for each child.

- Invite the children to dip their bread into the oil and taste it.

- **Say:** People have been eating olives for over two thousand years. I wonder what food we eat today—might still be eaten in two thousand years.

- **Say:** But Jesus did not go to the olive garden to eat olives. Jesus went to the garden to pray. Jesus was feeling sad, and he wanted to talk to God.

- **Ask:** When do you talk to God? Where do you like to go to talk to God?

- **Say:** Let's talk to God right now and thank God for this food. Thank you, God, for olives to taste. Amen.

adapted from PowerXpress! The Garden of Gethsemane © 2004 Abingdon Press

Prepare

✓ Provide the box decorated in Lesson 3.

Prepare

✓ Provide: varieties of olives, plain cream cheese, extra-virgin olive oil, crackers, crusty bread, paper plates, napkins, small bowls, small cups, spoons

✓ Cut the olives into small pieces and place the pieces in small bowls.

✓ Cut crusty bread into pieces.

- You can watch a 1:37 minute video about how olive oil is made today on You Tube: http://www.youtube.com/watch?v=IalTzb6z-YY&feature=related.

- You can see 15-second video of a Bible-times olive press on You Tube: http://www.youtube.com/watch?v=2FWWoEmntiI&feature=related.

NOTE: Websites are constantly changing. Although these websites were checked at the time this book was edited, we recommend that you double check the site to verify that it is still live and that it is still appropriate for children before doing the activity.

Make a Paper Prayer Garden

- Show the children a picture of van Gogh's painting, *The Olive Trees*.

- **Say:** Many artists paint pictures of trees and gardens. One famous artist, Vincent van Gogh, painted olive trees. His painting shows how olive trees have twisted trunks and branches. Let's make our own pictures of olive trees; but instead of using paint, we are going to use paper.

- Give each child a piece of light blue construction paper.

- Encourage the children to tear dark blue and purple scrap paper into shapes of mountains. Let the children glue the scraps onto the blue paper.

- Show the children how to tear brown paper into strips.

- Then show the children how to twist the strips to make them three-dimensional.

- Let the children glue the strips onto their construction paper in front of the mountains to make tree trunks and branches.

- Encourage the children to tear or cut green leaves to glue onto the trees.

- Let the children add white paper clouds and a green path if they wish.

- **Say:** After the Passover meal, Jesus and his friends went to the garden of Gethsemane, a garden of olive trees. Jesus went to the garden to pray.

- **Ask:** Have you ever prayed while you were outdoors? How do you think it would feel to pray while you were surrounded by trees?

- **Say:** We know that we can pray anytime and anywhere, but sometimes it is good to have a special place to go and pray.

- Set the pictures flat to dry. Plan to use the pictures again during worship.

Make Dish Prayer Gardens

- Cover the table with newspapers.

- **Say:** Jesus went to the garden of Gethsemane to pray. Let's make a dish garden to remind us of this Bible story.

- Give each child a shallow dish or container.

- Have the children line the bottom of the containers with small rocks.

- Next have the children add a layer of charcoal pieces.

- Finally have the children add a layer of potting soil. Let the children dampen the soil with water.

- Encourage the children to add small plants to their dish gardens.

- Show the children how to place the roots of the plants onto the soil and then make a mound of soil around the plants, covering the roots.

- Let the children add more soil to fill up the container.

- Have the children water the soil and mist the leaves of their plants.

Prepare

✓ Provide: light blue construction paper, a variety of paper scraps in different colors (especially green, brown, dark blue, and purple) and various textures (construction paper, tissue paper, paper cut from brown paper bags, and so forth), glue

✓ Provide: a print of Vincent Van Gogh, *The Olive Trees*. You can find the print in library books or online at: http://store.vangoghgallery.com/showprint.aspx?pid=25040.

NOTE: Websites are constantly changing. Although these websites were checked at the time this book was edited, we recommend that you double check the site to verify that it is still live and that it is still appropriate for children before doing the activity.

Prepare

✓ Provide: newspapers, shallow containers, small rocks or gravel, charcoal pieces, potting soil, water, water mister, small plants, spoons

Note: You may want the children to work together to make one large dish garden to display in the room rather than individual gardens.

Make Prayer Shawls

- Show the children a picture of a prayer shawl.

- **Say:** In our Bible story today Jesus went to a garden to pray. In Bible times Jewish men and boys over the age of thirteen wore a prayer shawl when they prayed. The prayer shawl is called a *tallith*. When a person puts on the *tallith* (TAH-lis), he says a blessing to God. Jesus probably wore a *tallith* when he prayed.

- Give each child a piece of fabric.

- **Say:** Sometimes the *tallith* had stripes of blue or black.

- Encourage the children to use markers to make stripes on their fabric.

- **Say:** At the bottom of the prayer shawl was a series of knots. Each knot was a reminder of one of the Ten Commandments. Jesus would have known these commandments.

- Help each child cut cord into four pieces: two 10-inch pieces and two 8-inch pieces.

- Help each child thread a piece of the 10-inch cord through a needle.

- Have the child push the piece through one corner of the cloth and knot the cord in place. Add three more knots to the cord. Repeat with the second 10-inch cord in the opposite corner of the cloth.

- Next have each child thread a piece of the 8-inch cord through a needle.

- Have the child push the piece through the third corner of the cloth and knot it in place. Tie two more knots in the cord. Repeat with the second 8-inch cord in the fourth corner of the fabric.

- Plan to use the prayer shawls during closing worship.

Prepare

✓ Provide: pre-washed muslin or old, white sheets; blue or black markers; yarn or cord; adult scissors; large-eyed needles

✓ Cut the fabric into 9- by 18-inch pieces for each child.

✓ You can find a picture of a prayer shawl at: http://commons.wikime dia.org/wiki/File:Prayer _Shawl.JPG

NOTE: *Websites are constantly changing. Although these websites were checked at the time this book was edited, we recommend that you double check the site to verify that it is still live and that it is still appropriate for children before doing the activity.*

Call for Help

- Have the children stand in a circle. Number the children. Make sure each child knows her or his number.

- Choose one child to be IT. IT stands in the center of the circle.

- **Say:** The object of the game is for IT to keep the balloon in the air. Anytime IT feels the need for help, he or she will yell, "Help!" and call out a number from one to (the number of children). That person will come to the center and try to help IT keep the balloon(s) off the floor. If a balloon hits the floor, IT will be replaced and the game will start all over again.

- Begin with one balloon and then add others.

- **Ask:** When there were more balloons than you could handle, what did you do? *(Call for help.)*

- **Say:** Jesus also called for help in today's Bible story. Jesus felt he needed help in order to do what God had called him to do.

Prepare

✓ Provide: balloons, plastic trash bag

✓ Blow up several balloons and place them in the trash bag.

adapted from Exploring Faith™ Middle Elementary, Teacher Spring 2001, © 2001 Cokesbury

Large Group

Bring all the children together to experience the Bible story. Tap a spoon on the side of a metal bowl or pan to alert the children to the large group time. Use the transition activity to move the children from the interest groups to the large group area.

Who's In the Garden?

- Have the children gather in the center of the room.

- **Say:** Today our Bible story is about Jesus praying in the garden of Gethsemane. After Jesus and his friends finished the Passover meal, they sang a hymn and then went to the garden. Jesus told his disciples to stay where they were. He asked three of his closest friends to go with him farther into the garden. He wanted his friends to watch and pray with him. The three friends were Peter, James, and John. We're going to play a game to help us remember Jesus and his three friends.

- Point to each corner of the room. Say the name posted in that corner. Have the children repeat the name.

- Choose a child to be the caller. The caller stands in the center of the room.

- **Say:** When I ask, "Who's in the garden?" our caller will close his or her eyes and count to ten. While the caller is counting, everyone else will run to one of the corners of the room. At the end of the counting, with eyes still closed, the caller will say the name of one of the people in the garden. All the children in that corner must sit in the center of the floor near the caller.

- Begin the game by asking, "Who's in the garden?"

- After the first round, stop the game and let the caller open his or her eyes.

- **Say:** This time when I ask the question, the caller will close his or her eyes again. Whoever is left in one of the corners may stay in their corner or move to another corner. But this time the children who are sitting down are going to sing a hymn so that our caller has trouble hearing which corner everyone is running to. You can sing "Jesus Loves Me" for the hymn.

- Begin the game again by asking, "Who's in the garden?" Encourage the seated children to sing "Jesus Loves Me."

- Continue the game until most of the children are seated.

adapted from PowerXpress! The Garden of Gethsemane, © 2004 Abingdon Press

Sleepy Time Theater

- Have the children sit down on the floor. If possible, scatter pillows around for the children to use while they are watching the play.

- Present the play, "In the Garden" to the children.

Prepare

✓ Provide: a spoon and a metal bowl or pan

✓ Provide: paper, marker, tape

✓ Make four signs. Write one of the following names on each sign: "Jesus, Peter, James, John"

✓ Tape one sign in each corner of the room.

Prepare

✓ Recruit older children, youth, or adults to be the narrator and the three mimes.

✓ Photocopy the script (page 43) for the actors.

✓ Provide: pillows for the children to relax on (optional)

Sign a Blessing

- **Say:** Jesus was sad and worried. He went to the garden to talk with God because he knew God would hear him. He knew God was with him no matter what happened. God is with you.

- Teach the children the signs for *God*, *with*, and *you* in American Sign Language.

- **God:** Point your index finger of your right hand, with the other fingers curled down. Bring the hand down and open the palm.

- **With:** Hold both hands in fists, with thumbs on the outside. Place the fists together, palms touching.

- **You:** point out with your index finger.

- Have the children turn to a friend and sign the blessing to each other.

Bible Verse Game

- **Say:** Our Bible verse today is Psalm 145:18: "The LORD is near to all who call on him."

- Have the children repeat the Bible verse.

- **Say:** In our Bible story today Jesus went to the garden of Gethsemane with his friends to pray. Jesus called on God because he was sad and feeling troubled. Repeat the Bible verse again, in a very sad voice.

- Have the children repeat the Bible verse in sad voices.

- **Say:** But Jesus knew that God was always with him. God is always with us.

- Place the words on the floor throughout the room. Secure each word with tape.

- **Say:** Let's play a game with the Bible verse to help us learn it. I will say the verse and leave out a word. I will throw the beach ball to someone. When that person catches the ball, he or she has to step on the missing word.

- Leave out words at random.

- If you have a large number of children, divide the children into smaller groups. Give each group a set of word cards and a ball.

Prepare

- ✓ Provide: adult scissors, tape, beach ball

- ✓ Photocopy and cut apart the Bible verse words (page 42).

- ✓ Tape the words on the floor around the room.

Small Groups

Divide the children into small groups. You may organize the groups around age levels or around readers and nonreaders. Keep the groups small, with a maximum of ten children in each group. You may need to have more than one of each group.

- Cover the table with newspapers or plastic and have the children wear paint smocks.

- **Say:** Jesus was sad and upset in today's Bible story.

- **Ask:** Have you ever felt sad or upset? Have you ever had to do something that you know will be hard to do?

- **Say:** Let's think about those feelings.

- Give each child a piece of fingerpaint paper and a paper plate.

- Place several blobs of different colors of fingerpaint on each plate.

- **Say:** I'm going to read some statements to you. I want you to use the fingerpaint to paint how you feel. You will do this activity in silence. I will be the only person talking.

- **Ask:** Is there someone special that you talk to? Who did Jesus talk to when he was sad and upset in today's Bible story? *(God)*

- Read the following statements to the children and let them paint. Pause in silence between each statement.

  > Sometimes I'm afraid of failing, but . . . "The LORD is near to all who call on him" (Psalm 145:18).

  > Sometimes I do things that I know are wrong, but . . . "The LORD is near to all who call on him" (Psalm 145:18).

  > Sometimes I feel like nobody understands me, but . . . "The LORD is near to all who call on him" (Psalm 145:18).

  > Sometimes I have to do things I don't want to do, but . . . "The LORD is near to all who call on him" (Psalm 145:18).

  > Sometimes I feel like no one is listening to me, but . . . "The LORD is near to all who call on him" (Psalm 145:18).

  > Sometimes someone hurts my feelings, but . . . "The LORD is near to all who call on him" (Psalm 145:18).

  > I know that I am not alone because . . . "The LORD is near to all who call on him" (Psalm 145:18).

- Set the painting aside to dry.

- Have the children wash their hands.

Prepare

✓ Provide: newspapers or plastic, smocks, fingerpaint paper, fingerpaints in different colors, hand-washing supplies, paper plates

Large-Group Worship

Bring everyone together for a time of closing worship.

- Teach the children to sing "The Lord Is Near" to the tune of "Good Is So Good." Sing the song several times.

The Lord Is Near

The Lord is near,
The Lord is near,
The Lord is near,
to all who call on him.

- Choose a child to bring the open Bible to the front of the room. Have the child place the Bible on the altar, or stand with the Bible while the Bible verse is said.

- **Say the Bible verse together with the children:** "The LORD is near to all who call on him" (Psalm 145:18).

- Quietly invite the children to put on their prayer shawls and pick up their olive garden pictures.

- Have the children find a spot in the room to sit down.

- Encourage the children to place their olive garden pictures on the floor in front of them.

- **Say:** *(Quietly)* Even though Jesus was sad and troubled, he knew he could talk to God. Jesus took his friends to the garden of Gethsemane, a special place where he could pray. You have made a special place to pray by yourself in this room. Spend the next few minutes silently talking to God.

    Thank God for your family . . .
    Thank God for your friends . . .
    Talk to God about a problem you might be having at school . . .
    Talk to God about a problem you might be having at home . . .
    Thank God for something that makes you happy . . .
    Know that God is always with you.

- Sign the blessing *God with you* with the children (see page 39) and then say, "Amen."

- Remind the children that they may still bring socks for "Bless My Sole."

Prepare

✓ Provide the olive garden pictures and the prayer shawls made earlier.

✓ Provide: a Bible

The LORD	is near
to all	**who**
call	**on him**
Psalm	**145:18**

24 Hours That Changed the World (For Younger Children)

In the Garden

(by Daphna Flegal)

Narrator: Supper was over. Jesus and his friends sang a hymn together and then left the upper room where they had celebrated the Passover. Jesus and his friends walked to a nearby garden, the garden of Gethsemane.

(Mimes stand and walk in place.)

Narrator: Jesus told his friends to sit down while he prayed.

(Mimes sit down.)

Narrator: Jesus asked Peter, James, and John to go with him farther into the garden. He wanted his three best friends to keep watch for him while he prayed.

(Mimes stand and walk in place.)

Narrator: Jesus stopped walking and turned to his friends.

(Mimes stop walking.)

Narrator: Jesus was feeling sad and worried. He needed to talk to God. He asked his friends to stay awake with him while he went even farther into the garden. It made him feel better to know his friends were watching over him.

(Mimes sit down.)

Narrator: Peter, James, and John loved Jesus. They wanted to help him. But it was getting late. Before long they began yawning. They could not keep their eyes open.

(Mimes stretch and yawn, then lie down, close their eyes, and start snoring.)

Narrator: While his three friends went to sleep, Jesus fell down on the ground and prayed to God. "Father," said Jesus. "I need your help. I don't want bad things to happen to me. I know you can do anything, so please don't let these bad things happen. But I know you are with me. And I will do whatever I need to do." Then Jesus got up and went back to his friends. They were still sleeping.

(Mimes are still snoring.)

Narrator: "Wake up!" said Jesus. "Wake up!"

(Mimes suddenly wake up.)

Narrator: "Couldn't you stay awake for even an hour?" asked Jesus. "You must stay awake and keep watch for me." Then Jesus left them and continued to pray. But his friends couldn't keep their eyes open.

(Mimes stretch and yawn, then lie down, close their eyes, and start snoring.)

Narrator: "Father," Jesus prayed again. "Please help me. I know you are with me. And I will do whatever I need to do." Once again Jesus got up and went back to his friends. Once again they were sleeping.

(Mimes are still snoring.)

Narrator: "Wake up!" said Jesus. "Wake up!"

(Mimes suddenly wake up.)

Narrator: Jesus was disappointed that his friends could not stay awake. But he was not done praying. He went back to pray one more time—and his friends went back to sleep.

(Mimes stretch and yawn, then lie down, close their eyes, and start snoring.)

Narrator: Jesus finished talking with God and returned to his friends—his very sleepy friends.

(Mimes are still snoring.)

Narrator: "Wake up!" said Jesus.

(Mimes suddenly wake up.)

Narrator: "Get up! said Jesus. "It's time. God has shown me what I must do."

(Mimes exit.)

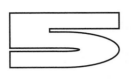

5 ARREST AND PETER'S DENIAL

Focus for the Teacher

Jesus' Arrest

When Jesus had finished praying in the garden of Gethsemane, he returned to Peter, James, and John and said that the hour had come. His betrayer was there.

Judas arrived in the garden along with a crowd armed with swords and clubs. It was a religious group, as the chief priests, scribes, and elders were present. Judas betrayed Jesus with a kiss. Jesus was arrested and, as he had predicted, was deserted by the disciples. But let us not be too hasty in condemning the disciples. They could not have helped Jesus; and because they survived, they were able to carry on his work.

Jesus was taken before the Council. Some people stood up and gave false testimony against him. Jesus did not answer his accusers, but stood silent.

> I don't even know the man you're talking about!
> Mark 14:71, CEV

Peter's Denial

Peter had followed Jesus from a distance and was in the courtyard below while Jesus was before the Council. A servant girl questioned him and said she thought he was with Jesus. Peter denied it. Again, bystanders said that Peter was with the Galilean, and he denied it. Just as Jesus had predicted, Peter denied Jesus three times before the cock crowed twice.

When Peter realized what had happened, he broke down and wept, for it was the one thing he had been sure he would not do. He had denied Jesus. To Peter's credit, this was the last time he denied Jesus. Peter became the strongest of the disciples and their spiritual leader after the Resurrection. Peter never again failed Jesus.

Bible Verse

We don't know for sure what Peter was thinking when he denied Jesus, but he was probably afraid of being arrested.

We Are Forgiven

Do we ever hide our identities as Christians because we are afraid of being conspicuous or being mocked? Remember Jesus forgave Peter and even asked Peter to be the leader of the disciples after the Resurrection. Peter learned from his mistakes and so can we. We are forgiven.

Explore Interest Groups

Be sure that adult leaders are waiting when the first child arrives. Greet and welcome each child. Get the child involved in an activity that interests him or her and introduces the theme for the day's activities.

Socks Box

- Thank any child who brought socks and place the socks in the box that was decorated during Lesson 3. Remind the children that they can still bring socks next week.

Rooster Prints

- Show the children the rooster lithograph from Picasso.

- **Say:** Picasso was a famous artist. He began painting when he was a child. He is especially famous for a type of art called cubism, but he actually made many different kinds of paintings, drawings, and sculptures — 20,000 in all. This picture shows a rooster. It is a kind of print called a lithograph. We're going to make a rooster print now.

- **Note:** The children may choose to draw their own roosters or try creating roosters using the art style of Picasso. The pattern on page 52 is optional.

- Give each child the rooster pattern. Have the child cut out the rooster.

- Have the child cut a square of sandpaper just slightly larger than the pattern of the rooster.

- Instruct each child to place the pattern on the sandpaper and draw around it using a thick pencil. Set the pattern to the side.

- **Say:** On the sandpaper choose a part of the body you want to cover with a particular color (for example, the head and tail might be orange; the feathers, feet, and waddle might be red; and the body and beak might be yellow). Color the chosen part of the body with crayons. Make sure you color with heavy lines.

- Let the children color their roosters.

- Set up an ironing board, or place a thick stack of folded newspapers on a tabletop while the children color.

- Plug in the iron. **CAUTION:** Be sure to keep the iron away from the children.

- Have the children come one at a time to the ironing station.

Prepare

✓ Provide the box decorated in Lesson 3.

Prepare

✓ Provide: safety scissors, sandpaper, thick pencils, crayons, iron, ironing board or newspapers

✓ Photocopy the rooster pattern (page 52).

✓ Provide a print of *Rooster* by Pablo Picasso. You may find the print in your public library or online.

- Place a piece of plain paper on the ironing board or newspapers. Place the sandpaper crayon-side facedown on top of the paper.

- Place the iron on the back of the sandpaper. Pick up the iron and move it to the next area of the sandpaper. Do <u>not</u> slide the iron over the paper (this will cause the crayon meltings to smear).

- Remove the sandpaper, and a print of the rooster will be transferred onto the paper.

- Let the print cool.

- Plan to use the rooster prints in small group time.

- **Say:** A rooster plays an important part in today's Bible story. We will find out why the rooster is so important at large group time.

Crowing Rooster

- **Say:** A rooster plays an important part in today's Bible story. Let's make roosters that can crow.

- Give each child a red plastic cup.

- Help each child use a pencil to poke a small hole in the bottom of the cup.

- Give each child a piece of yarn or cotton string and the rectangle of red felt. Show each child how to tie the string around the middle of the piece of red felt.

- Have each child thread the opposite end of the yarn or string down through the bottom of the cup. Pull the string until the felt is resting snugly against the bottom of the cup. This will make the rooster's comb.

- Encourage the children to decorate the cups to look like roosters. Let the children glue feathers on the sides of the cups to make wings.

- Give each child the felt triangle to make the beak and two google eyes. Encourage each child to glue the eyes and beak on the cup to complete the rooster.

- Show the children how to make the roosters crow. Give each child a small square of paper towel. Have the children dip the paper towels into water. Fold the wet paper towel tightly around the yarn or string. Drag the paper towel down the string in short jerky moves.

- Plan to use the rooster cups during large group time.

Rooster Crow Tag

- Move the children to an open area of the room.

- **Say:** A rooster plays an important part in today's Bible story. Let me hear you crow like a rooster.

- Encourage the children to crow like roosters.

- Play a game similar to Marco Polo.

Prepare

✓ Provide: red plastic cups (6 to 12 ounces), pencils, yarn or cotton string, paper towels, feathers, glue, google eyes, red felt and yellow or orange felt, shallow container partially filled with water, scissors

✓ Cut yarn or cotton string into 12-inch lengths. Cut red felt into 2- by 3-inch rectangles. Cut yellow felt into triangles about 2-inches across the base.

✓ You can get the idea of how this works by watching a YouTube video from ScienceBob that shows how to make a clucking chicken: http://www.youtube.com /watch?v=B8T80Eur8DI &feature=channel.

NOTE: Websites are constantly changing. Although these websites were checked at the time this book was edited, we recommend that you double check the site to verify that it is still live and that it is still appropriate for children before doing the activity.

Prepare

✓ Provide: scarf or sleep mask

- **Say:** In this game IT is one of Jesus' friends named Peter. IT will ask the question, "What's happening?" Everyone else must answer by crowing like a rooster.

- Choose a child to be IT. Guide IT to stand in the center of the room. Place a scarf or sleep mask over his or her eyes as a blindfold.

- Have IT count to ten and encourage the remaining children to move around.

- Then have IT ask the question, "What's happening?" IT may ask the question as often as he or she likes. The children must respond by crowing. IT will try to tag the children as they respond.

- When a child is tagged, that child must sit down until everyone is tagged.

Peter's Story Word Game

- **Say:** Our Bible story today is about Peter. There are several words in the story that may be unfamiliar to you. Let's look at these words.

- Give each child the pages of word tiles you photocopied before class.

- Let the children use safety scissors to cut out the word tiles.

- Have each child place one tile on the table or floor.

- Then have the child match each end of the tile (like dominoes) with the correct definition.

- Encourage the child to continue matching the word tiles.

- Discuss the words and the definitions with the children.

- **Say:** In our Bible story today, one of Jesus' friends, Judas, *betrayed* Jesus. He took money to lead the soldiers to Jesus.

- Have the child find the word *betray* and tell you the definition.

- **Say:** Jesus was *arrested*. Soldiers took him to the high priest's house.

- Have the child find the word *arrested* and tell you the definition.

- **Say:** Jesus is by himself. All his friends have *deserted* him.

- Have the child find the word *deserted* and tell you the definition.

- **Say:** Peter followed Jesus and the soldiers to the high priest's house, but he stayed in the courtyard. There were other *bystanders* in the courtyard.

- Have the child find the word *bystander* and tell you the definition.

- **Say:** One of the bystanders recognized Peter as a friend of Jesus. But Peter *lied*. He said he was not a friend of Jesus.

- Have the child find the word *lie* and tell you the definition.

- **Say:** Peter *denied* Jesus.

- Have the child find the word *deny* and tell you the definition.

Prepare

✓ Photocopy the word tiles (pages 52-53) for each child.

✓ Provide: safety scissors

Matches

lie: to tell something that is not true

deny: to say or believe that something is not true

arrested: to take someone by law

bystander: a person watching what is happening

deserted: to leave alone

betray: to give over to the enemy

Large Group

Bring all the children together to experience the Bible story. Tap a spoon on the side of a metal bowl or pan to alert the children to the large group time. Use the transition activity to move the children from the interest groups to the large group area.

Rooster Strut

- Have the children move to an open area of the room.

- Divide the children into teams. Have the teams line up on one side of the room.

- On the opposite side of the room, place a plastic tablecloth on the floor, then place a paper plate on the tablecloth for each team. Put a small amount of cereal on each plate.

- Have the first person from each team strut like a rooster to the paper plate. They might put their hands on their hips and flap their elbows like wings as they prance across the room.

- The child must kneel down and eat some of the cereal from the paper plate—without using his or her hands.

- Then the child struts back to the next person in line.

- While each child is walking back to the line, place a clean paper plate with cereal on the tablecloth for the next child. (Each child gets a new plate and new cereal).

- When the team is finished, everyone on the team crows like a rooster.

- Make sure the children understand the directions, then begin the game.

- **Say:** A rooster is important to today's Bible story. Let's find out why.

- Instruct the children to strut like a rooster as they move to sit down in the large group area.

Prepare

- ✓ Provide: a spoon and metal bowl or pan

- ✓ Provide: plastic tablecloth, paper plates, cereal

Red Rooster Theater

- Have the children sit down. Give them their crowing rooster cups.

- **Say:** As I tell the story, I want you to listen for the word *rooster*. Each time you hear the word rooster, make the crowing sound with your cups.

- Present the story, "Cock-a-doodle-doo!" (page 53) to the children.

Stand Up and Sign

- **Say:** Peter failed his friend when he said that he didn't know Jesus. Whenever we do things we shouldn't do, that is a way we say, "I don't know him!" But Peter never denied Jesus again. He learned to stand up for Jesus. Peter knew Jesus was his friend forever.

- Teach the children the signs for *Jesus* and *friend* in American Sign Language.

Prepare

- ✓ Provide crowing rooster cups made earlier.

- ✓ Locate today's Bible story, "Cock-a-doodle-doo!" (page 53)

- **Jesus:** Touch the middle finger of the right hand to the palm of the left hand. Reverse.

- **Friend:** Hook the right index finger over the left index finger. Reverse.

- **Say:** I'm going to tell a story about a boy or girl. Listen carefully. If the boy or girl in the story stands up for Jesus, then you stand up and sign the words *Jesus* and *friend* as you say, "Jesus is my friend."

Jesus

Friend

- **Story 1:** Chad's brother Jeremy got a new model airplane for his birthday. He worked very hard putting it together. One day while Jeremy was at basketball practice, Chad took the airplane without permission. He slipped it back into his brother's room before he got home.

- **Story 2:** A new family moved into the neighborhood. They had a boy the same age as Aiden. Aiden knew how it felt to be new, so he invited the new boy to sit with him on the bus and invited him to go to church with him.

- **Story 3:** Michelle saw a bracelet at the store. It would look great with her new outfit. She had already spent all her allowance for the week. When no one was looking, she slipped the bracelet into her back pack.

- **Story 4:** Erica was invited to go to a friend's house for a slumber party on Saturday night. Erica said, "I can go, but I have to leave in time to go to Sunday school and church on Sunday."

adapted from BibleZone™ 3 Younger Elementary, © 1998 Abingdon Press.

Bible Verse Prayer Litany

- **Say:** Our Bible verse today is Mark 14:71, CEV: "I don't even know the man you're talking about!"

- Have the children repeat the Bible verse.

- **Say:** Let's pray, asking God to forgive us when we do things that deny Jesus. I will say a statement and you respond with the Bible verse.

- **Pray:** God, sometimes we do things that are wrong. It's like we are saying,

- **Children:** "I don't even know the man you're talking about!"

- **Pray:** Forgive us when we make mistakes. We do not want to say,

- **Children:** "I don't even know the man you're talking about!"

- **Pray:** We know that Jesus is our friend forever. Help us stand up for Jesus. Amen.

Small Groups

Divide the children into small groups. You may organize the groups around age levels or around readers and nonreaders. Keep the groups small, with a maximum of ten children in each group. You may need to have more than one of each group.

- **Say:** Peter cried when he heard the rooster crow and realized what he had done. He was sorry for what he had done. The Bible tells us more about what happened to Peter. Let's look up Peter's story in our Bibles. Turn in your Bibles to John 21:15.

- Help the children find the verse.

- **Say:** This part of Peter's story happened after the Resurrection.

- **Ask:** What did Jesus ask Peter? *(Do you love me?)* What was Peter's answer? *(Yes)*

- **Ask:** What are some things we can do to show Jesus that we love him? *(come to church, treat people kindly, share food with people who are hungry, share clothes with people in need, invite a friend to come to church, read my Bible, sing in the children's choir, and so forth)*

- Encourage the children to brainstorm ideas. Write their ideas on newsprint.

- Hand out the rooster prints that the children made earlier in the lesson.

- **Ask:** Could you promise to do one of these things this next week? Which one?

- **Say:** Write that idea underneath your rooster print.

- When the children have finished writing, have the children place their prints in front of them.

- **Say:** Let's pray. As we pray, we will take turns saying what we promise to do to show love to Jesus. If you don't want to share what you promised, just turn your print over and we will know to go on to the next person.

- **Pray:** God, sometimes we do things that are wrong. But we know you forgive us. We want to show our love for you by: *(Encourage each child to name the idea he or she wrote on his or her print.)*

- **Pray:** We know that Jesus is our friend forever. Help us stand up for Jesus. Amen.

- Have the children take their prints with them to large group worship.

Prepare
✓ Provide: Bibles, newsprint, markers, rooster prints made earlier

Large-Group Worship

Bring everyone together for a time of closing worship.

- Teach the children to sing "Peter Heard the Rooster Crow" to the tune of "Do You Know the Muffin Man?"

Peter Heard the Rooster Crow

Peter, do you know this man,
Know this man, know this man?
Peter, do you know this man?
He is your friend.

No, I do not know this man,
Know this man, know this man.
No, I do not know this man,
He is not my friend.

Peter heard the rooster crow,
The rooster crow, the rooster crow.
Peter heard the rooster crow,
(crow like a rooster).

Peter cried, he was so sad,
Was so sad, was so sad.
Peter cried, he was so sad,
When the rooster crowed.

© 2001 Abingdon Press

- Choose a child to bring the open Bible to the front of the room. Have the child place the Bible on the altar, or stand with the Bible while the Bible verse is said.

- **Say the Bible verse together with the children:** "I don't even know the man you're talking about!" (Mark 14:71, CEV).

- **Say:** Peter was sorry he said he did not know Jesus. The Bible tells us that after the Resurrection, Peter got to tell Jesus that he loved him. Bring your rooster prints to the front to help us remember ways we can show Jesus that we love him.

- Have the children bring their rooster prints and place them on the altar or at the front of the room.

- **Say:** Peter never denied Jesus again. He knew Jesus was his friend forever.

- Sign *Jesus is my friend* with the children (see page 49).

- **Pray:** Thank you, God, for forgiving us when we act like we do not know Jesus. Help us show our love for Jesus every day. Amen.

- Remind the children that they may still bring socks for "Bless My Sole."

Prepare

✓ Provide the rooster prints made earlier.

✓ Provide: a Bible

lie

to take
someone
by law

deny

to give over
to the
enemy

arrested

to say or
believe that
something
is not true

24 Hours That Changed the World (For Younger Children)

Cock-a-doodle-doo!

by Sharilyn S. Adair

On the night that he ate his last meal with his friends, Jesus said something that surprised them all, particularly Peter. After everyone had finished eating, Jesus said, "You will all become deserters."

Everyone was upset, especially Peter. How could Jesus even imagine that he would be a deserter? No way! So Peter jumped to his feet.

"Even if everyone else deserts you, I won't!" said Peter. "You can count on me!"

But Jesus just shook his head sadly as he looked at his friend. "Peter, tonight you will tell people three different times that you do not even know who I am. And you will do this before the **rooster** crows twice." *(Pause to let the children make their cups crow.)*

Later that night Judas led the soldiers to the garden where Jesus had been praying. The leaders had paid Judas a bag of silver to betray Jesus, his friend and teacher. The soldiers arrested Jesus. What do you think his friends did? They all ran away as fast as they could, even Peter. No one stayed to help Jesus.

The soldiers took Jesus to the house of the high priest. Peter followed, hiding in the shadows. He crept into the courtyard of the house. He saw some guards warming their hands around a campfire. Peter eased among them. He wanted to know what was going on. He hoped no one would recognize him. Peter had forgotten what Jesus had said about the **rooster** crowing. *(Pause to let the children make their cups crow.)*

At first nobody noticed Peter. Then one of the servant girls came by. She looked at Peter. "Don't I know you? You were with Jesus!"

"I don't know what you are talking about," he said. Just then a **rooster** crowed. *(Let the children make crowing sounds with their cups.)*

Peter tried to disappear into the crowd that had gathered. But the servant girl followed him. She started telling the bystanders, "This is one of Jesus' friends. I know it."

"No! You are wrong," lied Peter. "I don't know him."

A bystander looked more closely at Peter. "I think you are one of his friends. You talk like one of them!"

Peter shouted, "I don't know this man you are talking about!" And for the second time that night the **rooster** crowed. *(Let the children make crowing sounds with their cups.)*

At that moment Peter remembered what Jesus had said: "Before the **rooster** crows twice, you will deny me three times." *(Let the children make crowing sounds with their cups.)*

Peter put his head in his hands and cried.

adapted from Bible Zone 3 Younger Elementary © 1998 Abingdon Press

betray	a person watching what's happening

bystander	to leave alone

deserted	to tell something that is not true

6 GOOD FRIDAY

Objectives
The children will
- hear Mark 15:1-41;
- recognize that Jesus is truly God's Son;
- discover that the day Jesus died is called Good Friday;
- learn that the cross helps us remember God's great love for us;
- continue the service project.

Bible Story
Mark 15:1-41: Jesus' trial, crucifixion, and death

Bible Verse
Mark 15:39: Truly this man was God's Son!

Focus for the Teacher

Jesus on Trial

The Jewish religious leaders didn't just want to arrest Jesus; they wanted to get rid of him permanently. However, only the Romans could execute people. So the Jewish leaders had to enlist the Romans in their plot to condemn Jesus. They arranged for witnesses to testify falsely to what they had seen and heard from Jesus, and they manipulated Pilate. All of this ensured that Jesus would be condemned to die. And certainly the crowd was stacked against him, when the mob clamored for Barabbas, a rebel leader and murderer, rather than Jesus.

> Truly this man was God's Son!
> Mark 15:39

Good Friday

The deed was done. Jesus was in Roman custody and condemned to die. He was mocked and scourged and humiliated. Then he was crucified on the day before the sabbath, a day we call "Good Friday." Many people wonder what is "good" about Good Friday. The "good" reflects God's accomplishment—showing God's unconditional love—through Jesus' death.

Bible Verse

This verse is the dramatic confession by the centurion who watched the Jesus' crucifixion. After he saw how Jesus died, he realized that Jesus was indeed God's Son.

The Children

The details of Jesus' crucifixion are missing from today's lesson. These stories are told to impress upon adults the excruciating pain Jesus suffered and the sacrifice that Jesus made for our redemption. These stories might frighten young, impressionable children. Also, rather than understand the supreme sacrifice Jesus made, children might focus instead on the blood and violence surrounding Jesus' death.

We want them to understand that Jesus was put to death not because he was a bad person, but because people did not understand what his message was all about. We want them to understand that Jesus chose to endure a terrible death as a way to ensure our salvation. We want them to know the story, but we don't want to distract the children with details that may or may not add to the story.

adapted from Exploring Faith™ Middle Elementary, Teacher, Spring, © 2002 Cokesbury

Explore Interest Groups

Be sure that adult leaders are waiting when the first child arrives. Greet and welcome each child. Get the child involved in an activity that interests him or her and introduces the theme for the day's activities.

Socks Box

- Thank any child who brought socks and place the socks in the box that was decorated in Lesson 3. Remind the children that they have one more week to bring socks for "Bless My Sole."

Remembering Good Friday

- **Say:** Today our Bible story is about the day Jesus died. Jesus was crucified on a cross. It was a terrible day, but we call this day *Good Friday*.

- **Ask:** Why do you think Christians call the day Jesus was crucified *Good Friday*?

- **Say:** We call it *Good Friday* because we know that the story does not end with Jesus' death on the cross. We know that Jesus rose from the dead. The cross reminds us of God's love for us.

    The day Jesus died may have first been called God's Friday. *Good* is an Old English word for *holy*, so the day can also be called Holy Friday.

    Jesus was God's promised Messiah to the Jewish people. Some thought that the Messiah was for the Jewish people only. But Roman soldiers, who were not Jews, stood at the foot of the cross and said, "Truly this man was God's Son."

    Christians know that the good news of God's love through Jesus is good news for all people. Jesus made the journey to the cross for everyone. The story did not end with Jesus' death. God raised Jesus from the dead. Jesus is the living Christ. Through Jesus, God offers new life to all people.

    The empty cross is a symbol of Good Friday. It helps us remember how much God loves us.

- Explain to the children that there are several activity stations set up around the room. At each station they will be able to make a different kind of cross.

- The children may take all their crosses home, or they may want to keep only one cross and give the others to friends and family members as a way to remember Good Friday.

    adapted from PowerXpress!® Bible Experience Stations® Journey to the Cross © 2001 Abingdon Press

Prepare

✓ Provide the box decorated in Lesson 3.

Prepare

✓ Set up the stations for each activity. The supplies are listed with each activity.

Icing Hot Cross Buns

- Put out enough buns or rolls for everyone to have one. Keep a basic sugar icing warm in a slow cooker.

- **Say:** Eating hot cross buns on Good Friday is a tradition of the Christian church that goes back a long time. It symbolizes Jesus' death on the cross. We are going to ice buns for everyone. Spread the warm icing in the form of a cross.

- Make sure the children use hand sanitizer to clean their hands.

- Give everyone a plastic or butter knife.

- Have them spread icing on each bun in the form of a cross.

- Have them put the finished buns on napkins or small plates and then put them on trays for serving later during small group time.

Beaded Crosses

- Give each child an 18-inch shoelace.

- *Step 1:* Show the child how to thread the shoelace with one pony bead and move the bead to the center point of the shoelace.

- *Step 2:* Have the child lace both ends of the lace through another pony bead. Push the single bead snugly against the first bead.

- *Steps 3 & 4:* Have the child thread the right lace through another bead, the left lace through a fourth bead, then thread the two ends through a fifth bead.

- *Step 5:* Show the child how to pull the lace tight, then insert a sixth bead between the two side beads, then push down snugly to hold the interior bead in place.

- *Step 6:* Help the child tie the ends together.

Clay and Bead Crosses

- Let the children work together to make salt dough.

- Combine 4 cups flour and 1 cup salt in a large mixing bowl. Gradually add in 2 to 2½ cups warm water. Mix thoroughly.

- Give each child a portion of the dough to knead.

- Let the children add color to their dough.

- Pour liquid tempera onto each ball of dough.

- Have the child fold over the dough with the paint inside the fold.

- Instruct the child to knead the dough until it is colored throughout.

- Have each child flatten and roll out the dough until it is about ½ inch thick.

Prepare

✓ Provide: enough plain buns or rolls for each person to have one, and enough warm icing

✓ Set up a slow cooker containing a simple sugar icing to warm.

✓ Provide: hand sanitizer, small plates or napkins, serving trays, plastic or butter knives

Prepare

✓ Provide: 18-inch shoelaces (preferably leather), 6 pony beads per cross

Prepare

✓ Provide: flour, salt, warm water, mixing bowl, measuring cups, mixing spoon, rolling pins, wax paper, cross cookie cutter, several colors of *liquid* tempera paints, pony beads, paper clips, permanent marker

Note: If time is short, prepare the dough before class. Place the dough in an airtight container. Store in the refrigerator.

- Let the children take turns using the cookie cutter to cut out crosses.

- Give each child a piece of wax paper. Use a permanent marker to write each child's name on the wax paper.

- Help the child place the clay cross on the wax paper.

- Give each child a paper clip.

- Show the child how to place the paper clip in about halfway up the back to make a hanger.

- Encourage each child to choose from the available pony beads and press the beads into the clay cross however he or she wishes. The beads need to pushed firmly into the dough.

- Set the crosses aside to dry. Store them somewhere that they can safely stay until next week.

Craft Stick Crosses

- Give each child the longer rectangle. This rectangle will make the long base of the cross.

- Have the child write his or her name on the back of the rectangle.

- Have each child glue four craft sticks side-by-side across the rectangle. The sticks should be lined up at one end of the rectangle. The sticks can overhang the edge of the rectangle a little bit.

- Have each child glue four more craft sticks side-by-side across the remaining part of the rectangle. These will need to overlap the first four craft sticks. *(An example of this cross is on the cover of this Leader's Guide).*

- Give each child the shorter rectangle. This will make the cross bar.

- Have each child glue four craft sticks side-by-side across the shorter rectangle. The sticks may overhang the edge of the rectangle a little bit.

- Have the children glue the shorter piece across the longer piece about one-fourth of the way from the top.

- Set the crosses aside to dry.

Folk Art Crosses

- **Say:** In some countries, like Mexico, people make folk art crosses. These crosses are very colorful and often have scenes from Jesus' life painted on them.

- Show the children an example of a folk art cross.

- Set out art paper and a variety of brightly colored crayons or markers.

- Have the children use a pencil to draw a cross shape as large as the paper will allow.

- Have the children trace the shape with a dark crayon or marker.

- Encourage the children to draw scenes from Jesus' life inside the cross. These might include Jesus' birth, the visit of the wise men, Jesus' baptism, calling the disciples, talking with children, and so forth.

Prepare

✓ Provide: adult scissors, 12 craft sticks per child, glue, markers, cardboard or posterboard

✓ Cut one rectangle 1½ inches by 4 inches and another rectangle 1½ inches by 6 inches from posterboard or cardboard for each child.

Prepare

✓ Provide: art paper, brightly colored crayons or markers, dark crayons or markers, pencils

Note: An example of a folk art cross may be found in books from the public library or on the Internet at: http://www.worldfolkart.or g/category.php?id=37&sub_ id=385.

NOTE: Websites are constantly changing. Although these websites were checked at the time this book was edited, we recommend that you double check the site to verify that it is still live and that it is still appropriate for children before doing the activity.

Large Group

Bring all the children together to experience the Bible story. Tap a spoon on the side of a metal bowl or pan to alert the children to the large group time. Use the transition activity to move the children from the interest groups to the large group area.

Symbol Snatch

- Have the children move to the large group area.

- Give each child a set of cross trading cards.

- Have the children cut out the individual cards. Then collect the scissors and throw away the scraps.

- **Say:** These cards show different kinds of crosses. Today our Bible story is about the day Jesus died. Jesus was crucified on a cross. It was a terrible day.

- **Ask:** So why do you think the cross is a symbol for Jesus? Why do we put the cross in our church?

- **Say:** Jesus died because he wanted to show his friends how much God loved them. *We* are Jesus' friends. Jesus died to show *us* how much God loves *us*. The cross helps us remember this.

- **Say:** Look at each of these crosses. Each one is empty. The empty cross helps us remember that Jesus' death is not the end of the story. God raised Jesus from the dead.

- **Say:** I want you to choose one set of crosses to collect. For example, you might want to collect all the crosses that look like anchors. What you will do is offer to trade with other boys and girls in the room until you have all of the anchor crosses. When you have ten (or the number of children playing if you have less than ten) of one kind, then sit down in our large group area.

- Begin by saying, "Go!" Continue until most of the children are seated.

adapted from BibleZone™ 3 Younger Elementary © 1998 Abingdon Press

Prepare

✓ Provide: spoon and a metal bowl or pan

✓ Photocopy the crosses (page 62) for each child.

✓ Provide: safety scissors

Taste and See Theater

- **Note:** You may want to do this large group activity in a different room around tables. This would allow you to set up for the story ahead of time.

- Place a purple plastic cloth on the floor (or table) for each group of no more than eight children.

- Arrange the various foods in cups or on plates and place them in the center of the table.

- **Say:** We have been learning about what happened to Jesus during the last week of his life here on earth. We call that week Holy Week. Let's review what happened during Holy Week.

- Tell the children the story "A Faithful Journey" and encourage the children to taste the foods as indicated in the story.

Prepare

✓ Provide for each group of children: purple plastic tablecloth, plates or cups, dates, matzoh, pretzels (not pretzel sticks), sunflower seeds

✓ Photocopy the script (page 63) for the storyteller.

Sign a Truth

- **Say:** Jesus died on the cross so that we would know how much God loves us.

- Teach the children the signs for *God*, *loves*, and *me* in American Sign Language.

- **God:** Point your index finger of your right hand, with the other fingers curled down. Bring the hand down and open the palm.

- **Loves:** Cross your hands at the wrists and press them over your heart.

- **Me:** Point to yourself with your index finger.

Bible Verse Game

- **Say:** Our Bible verse today is: "Truly this man was God's Son!" (Mark 15:39)

- Have the children repeat the Bible verse.

- Instruct the children to help you set up a circle of chairs. You will need one chair for each child. If you have a large number of children, set up more than one circle.

- Invite the children to sit in the chairs.

- **Say:** Let's play a game. One of you will be the Roman centurion. You will stand in the center of the circle. The Roman centurion will say, *"Truly this man was ..."* and fill in the blank. Whenever you hear the Bible verse completed, *"Truly this man was God's Son!"* then you have to change places around the circle. While you are changing places, the Roman centurion will try to capture you and put you in the Roman prison (the center of the circle). Whoever is captured, sits in the center of the circle, and his or her chair is removed from the circle. When everyone is in the center, the game is over.

- Suggest phrases such as: *"Truly this man was God's (cousin, uncle, grandfather, nephew, next door neighbor, and so forth)."*

- Choose one child in each circle to be the centurion. Have that child move to the center of the circle and take away his or her chair.

- Play the game until everyone is in the center of their circle.

adapted from BibleZone™ 7 Younger Elementary © 1999 Abingdon Press

Prepare

✓ Provide: a chair for each child

Small Groups

Divide the children into small groups. You may organize the groups around age levels or around readers and nonreaders. Keep the groups small, with a maximum of ten children in each group. You may need to have more than one of each group.

- Have the children sit down in your small group area.

- Serve the hot cross buns made earlier.

- **Say:** Eating hot cross buns on Good Friday is a tradition of the Christian church that goes back a long time. It symbolizes Jesus' death on the cross.

- Say a thank-you prayer.

- Let everyone eat. Have hand wipes or hand-washing supplies available to clean sticky hands.

- Give each child a section of the coffee filter, a marker, two pieces of the plastic report covers that you cut ahead, two paper clips, and a jar lid.

- Instruct the children to place the coffee filter wedges so that the point faces down in front of them on the table.

- Have each child use the marker to draw a cross on the wedge.

- Have the child place the drawing between the two pieces of plastic, with the point touching the bottom edge of the plastic.

- Show the child how to roll the plastic-encased drawing into a cylinder 1½ inches in diameter. Help each child secure the cylinder with a paper clip at the top and a paper clip at the bottom.

- Have the child stand the cylinder in the jar lid with the point of the filter paper at the bottom.

- When every child has a cylinder standing in a jar lid, fill each jar lid with water.

- **Say:** You drew a black cross. The sky turned black the day Jesus died. Darkness covered the whole city of Jerusalem. A great earthquake shook the city. The veil in the Jerusalem Temple was torn from top to bottom. But the cross is not the end of the story. Watch what happens to the cross you drew as the filter paper gets wet.

- **Ask:** Do you see anything changing? (The black cross is disappearing. Other colors are appearing—probably pink, blue, and yellow.)

- **Say:** As we looked at our cross, we could see more than our drawing. We could see the different colors hidden in the black ink. As Christians we look at the cross and see more than two pieces of wood. We look at the cross and know that there was more to the story. We remember that Jesus rose from the dead. We remember that Jesus shows us how much God loves us. We remember that Jesus offers new life to us.

adapted from PowerXpress!® Bible Experience Stations® Journey to the Cross © 2001 Abingdon Press

Prepare

✓ Provide: the hot cross buns made earlier, napkins, plates, hand-washing supplies

✓ Provide: round coffee filters, scissors, black watercolor felt-tip markers, clear plastic report covers, paper clips, plastic jar lids (mayonnaise or peanut butter jar lids work well), water

✓ Cut the coffee filters into pie-shaped wedges (eight wedges per filter).

✓ Cut plastic report covers into 4½- by 5½- inch pieces for each child.

Note: This experiment will not work with permanent markers.

24 Hours That Changed the World (For Younger Children)

Large-Group Worship

Bring everyone together for a time of closing worship.

- Have the children gather their crosses and place them nearby, ready to take home.

- Teach the children to sing "Truly This Man" to the tune of "God Is So Good." Sing the song several times.

Truly This Man

Truly this man, truly this man,
Truly this man, this man was God's Son!

- Choose a child to bring the open Bible to the front of the room. Have the child place the Bible on the altar, or stand with the Bible while the Bible verse is said.

- **Say the Bible verse together with the children:** "Truly this man was God's Son!" (Mark 15:39).

- Sign *God loves you* with the children (see page 59).

- Light the seven candles and darken the room.

- **Say:** We will end our worship with a service of darkness. We will remember the events of Good Friday and blow out each candle. The room will get darker and darker. After the prayer, we will leave the room in silence.

- Choose seven children to come forward and blow out the candles.

- **Candle One:** Judas led the soldiers to Jesus. He betrayed Jesus with a kiss. The soldiers arrested Jesus. *(Extinguish candle one.)*

- **Candle Two:** They took Jesus to the high priest's house. Peter followed, but he denied knowing Jesus three times. Then the rooster crowed. *(Extinguish candle two.)*

- **Candle Three:** At the home of the high priest, they decided that Jesus should die. *(Extinguish candle three.)*

- **Candle Four:** When morning came, they took Jesus to Pilate. *(Extinguish candle four.)*

- **Candle Five:** Pilate did not think Jesus deserved to die. But the crowd wanted Pilate to crucify Jesus. *(Extinguish candle five.)*

- **Candle Six:** Pilate did what the crowd wanted. He handed Jesus over to be crucified. *(Extinguish candle six.)*

- **Candle Seven:** Jesus died. When the Roman centurion saw how Jesus died he said, "Truly this man was God's Son!" *(Extinguish candle seven.)*

- **Pray:** Thank you, God, for your Son, Jesus. We are amazed at your great love for us. Amen.

- Encourage the children to leave in silence.

Prepare

✓ Provide: a Bible, seven candles, matches or lighter (*for leader's use only*)

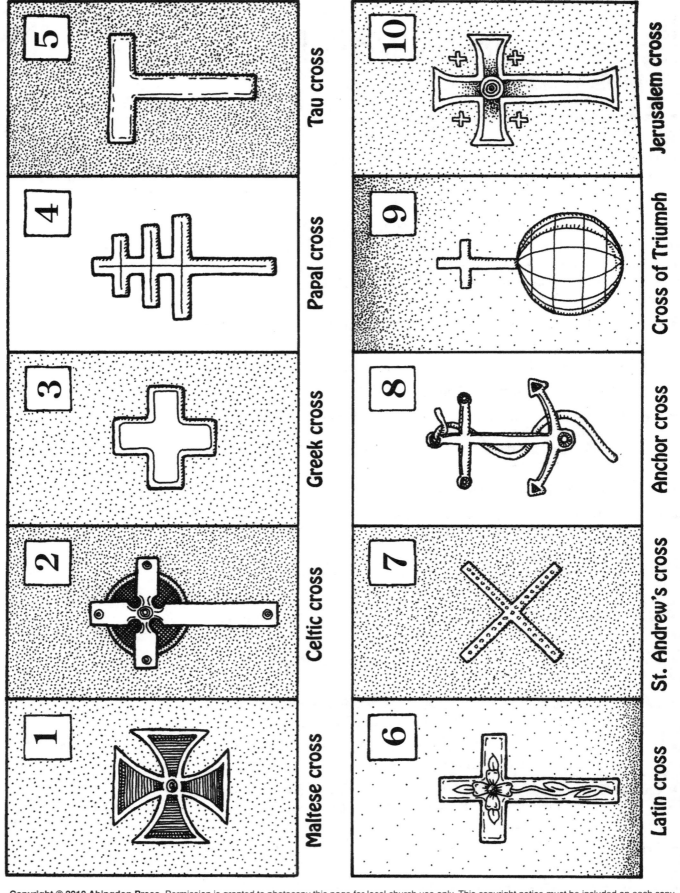

5 Tau cross

4 Papal cross

3 Greek cross

2 Celtic cross

1 Maltese cross

10 Jerusalem cross

9 Cross of Triumph

8 Anchor cross

7 St. Andrew's cross

6 Latin cross

24 Hours That Changed the World (For Younger Children)

A Faithful Journey
based on the story by Joyce Brown

The first Sunday of Holy Week was a joyful day. Jesus entered the city in peace, riding on a donkey. People lined the roadside, hoping to get a glimpse of Jesus. Some took off their cloaks and laid them on the road. "Hosanna!" they shouted. Others tore palm branches from the trees and waved the branches joyfully.

Those palm branches may have come from date palms, so we begin our story with dates. *(Serve the dates.)*

Thursday, near sundown, Jesus and his twelve disciples entered a borrowed house. Here they ate the Passover meal together.

Jesus asked his friends to remember him when they ate bread and drank wine together. *(Serve the matzoh.)*

After supper Jesus and the disciples went to the garden of Gethsemane.

In the quiet of that garden, while his disciples fell asleep, Jesus prayed. "Please, my Father, I don't want to go through what's about to happen to me. But I want to do what you need me to do. I know you will be with me. So, whatever you wish me to do, I will do—no matter how hard it is."

(Hold up a pretzel.) If we look at the shape of a pretzel, we see arms folded in prayer. *(Serve the pretzels.)*

Suddenly a large crowd came out of the darkness. Judas, one of the disciples, was leading them! As Judas greeted Jesus with a kiss, the crowd arrested Jesus.

The soldiers led him from the dark garden to the home of the high priest, where the leaders of the Jewish people had assembled.

Peter followed Jesus and the soldiers to the courtyard of the high priest. As people in the courtyard recognized Peter, he denied even knowing Jesus. And then the rooster crowed twice. Peter wept as he realized he had deserted his friend.

Inside the high priest's house the Jewish leaders decided Jesus deserved to die; but Rome ruled the country. Only Roman officials could sentence Jesus to death.

Early on Friday they led Jesus to Pilate, the Roman governor. Pilate listened to the charges against Jesus, but he did not believe that Jesus should be killed.

"Remember, it is my custom at Passover time to release a prisoner," said Pilate, "Which prisoner do you want me to set free—the notorious prisoner, Jesus Barabbas, or this Jesus who is called the Messiah?"

"Release Barabbas," cried the crowd.

"Then what should I do with Jesus?"

"Crucify him," cried the crowd. And Pilate decided to do as they demanded.

So Jesus began the long, lonely walk toward the hill where he would die.

By afternoon darkness covered the city. Then Jesus died. The ground trembled, and the curtain in the Temple was torn from top to bottom. In the darkness the disciples of Jesus hid, for they had all deserted their friend.

In the darkness women stood at a distance, gazing toward their crucified Messiah.

In the darkness a Roman soldier stood at the foot of the cross and whispered, "Truly this man was God's Son!"

(Hold up a sunflower seed.) Seeds contain new life. We bury seeds in the ground, believing that the seed will be transformed into a new plant. Jesus' journey to the cross offered new life. Jesus rose from the dead. Through Jesus, God offers new life to the whole world. *(Serve the sunflower seeds.)*

adapted from PowerXpress!® Journey to the Cross © 2001 Abingdon Press

7 THE RESURRECTION

Objectives
The children will
- hear Mark 16:1-6;
- realize that Jesus is alive and always with us;
- respond to the Easter story with joy.

Bible Story
Mark 16:1-8: The empty tomb

Bible Verse
Mark 16:6: He has been raised; he is not here.

Focus for the Teacher

Jesus' Triumph Over Death

The tone of today's lesson will be very different from the sadness of the preceding lessons. We have gone through Jesus' triumphal entry into Jerusalem arrest, trial, and finally his crucifixion and death.

In the Gospel of Mark three women came to the tomb on Sunday, the first day of the week. They went to perform the customary burial rites that they had not been allowed to do because of the timing of Jesus' death so close to the sabbath. Jewish custom forbade embalming, so a dead body was washed, rubbed with perfumes and spices, and wrapped in a shroud. Touching a dead body rendered the caretaker unclean until purification rituals were performed. So, consequently the rituals of burial could not be performed for Jesus until after the sabbath was over.

When the women came to the garden, they saw that the stone that had sealed Jesus' tomb was moved. They were alarmed when they saw a young man in a white robe who told them that Jesus had been raised. Jesus had told them he would rise, but they had seen him die and did not have Jesus' understanding of the ways of God.

> He has been raised; he is not here.
> Mark 16:6

Bible Verse

When the women saw the young man in the white robe, they reacted with fear. When they heard the young man's message, they were even more afraid.

In fact, when they fled from the tomb they told no one what they had seen and heard. They were unprepared for the new reality: Jesus was alive!

Easter Sunday

Easter is the highlight of the Christian Year, a day of great celebration for Christians. Jesus is alive! It is a time to celebrate new life in all its forms. Children may, at Easter, have a great number of questions about the Resurrection. Answer their questions as simply and as honestly as possible. As adults, we still don't have all the answers. It's perfectly acceptable to say, "I don't know." What we do know is that with God, all things are possible.

Remind the children that Easter is a day when we are reminded over and over again just how much God truly loves us. God held nothing back, not even God's only Son, in order to give us eternal life.

Signs of New Life

Help the children make the connection between Easter and the symbols they see all around them. For example, the custom of getting new clothes for Easter comes from the early converts to the new church who put on new white robes as a symbol of their new life. Easter eggs and baby animals symbolize the new life that Jesus brings to us.

Explore Interest Groups

Be sure that adult leaders are waiting when the first child arrives. Greet and welcome each child. Get the child involved in an activity that interests him or her and introduces the theme for the day's activities.

Socks Box

- Thank any child who brought socks and place the socks in the box.

- Have the children prepare the socks for mailing. Let the children take turns placing the socks in the mailing boxes you have provided.

- Tape the boxes shut and address to:
Bless My Sole, Centenary United Methodist Church
411 E. Grace St.
Richmond, VA 23219

Set Design

- Have the children design the set for today's theater presentation.

- Cut a piece of mural paper large enough to make a backdrop for your presentation area.

- Outline a rounded shape to represent the tomb. Outline a rounded doorway inside the larger shape.

- To the side of the tomb outline draw the outline of the large stone that was rolled in front of the tomb.

- Mount the mural as the backdrop to your presentation area.

- **Say:** Our Bible story today is about the first Easter morning. After Jesus died, a man named Joseph took him down from the cross, wrapped him in strips of cloth, and laid Jesus' body in a tomb. The tomb was carved of rock. Inside the tomb a shelf was carved. The body was laid on the shelf. After the body was placed in the tomb, a large round stone was rolled in front of the opening to seal the tomb closed. We will need a tomb for our large group time. You will be set designers and make the garden tomb.

- Have the children decorate the tomb and stone outlines by painting with tempera paint or by adding strips of duct tape.

- If you choose to let the children paint, cover the floor in front of the mural with a drop cloth or newspapers and have the children wear smocks.

- The children may make the backdrop three dimensional by crumpling gray paper into loose balls and then taping the balls inside the outline using loops of duct tape.

- Let the children add plants to the presentation area if you have some available.

Prepare

✓ Provide: mailing boxes, mailing tape, address labels, marker

Prepare

✓ Provide: mural paper, adult scissors, markers, duct tape, gray paper, gray tempera paint, brushes, hand-washing supplies, smocks, drop cloth or newspapers, real or artificial plants (optional)

An Egg-cellent Symbol

- Cover the table with a plastic tablecloth or with newspaper.

- Have the children wear smocks to protect their clothing.

- Give each child a coffee filter and a pencil.

- Have the children draw an egg shape as large as the coffee filter will allow.

- Instruct the children to cut out the coffee filter egg.

- **Say:** The egg became a symbol of Easter a long, long, time ago. Before Jesus was even born, eggs were a common springtime gift. They reminded people of the new life of spring. Then the Christian church adopted the giving of eggs. For the forty days of Lent, however, the church forbid people to eat eggs. But no one told the chickens; they kept on laying eggs. Soon there were many more eggs than the people needed. So people started to decorate them and give them as gifts. Today we dye Easter eggs in joyful colors because we remember that Jesus rose from the dead.

adapted from BibleZone™ 7 Younger Elementary © 1999 Abingdon Press

- Place the containers of colored water on the table for the children to share.

- Give each child a drinking straw.

- Show the children how to dip a straw into the colored water and cover the end of the straw with a finger so the colored water stays in it.

- Then hold the straw over the egg shape. Remove your finger from the end of the straw to release the colored water onto the egg. The filter paper will cause the colors to spread.

- Encourage the children to repeat the process with different colors.

- Have paper towels on hand to immediately clean up any spills.

- Set the colorful eggs flat to dry.

Easter Surprise

- Have the children wear smocks as they will be using permanent markers.

- Give each child a plastic Easter egg.

- Hold up the empty plastic egg. *(Keep the egg closed.)*

- **Say:** The Easter egg is a symbol of Easter. We dye eggs in joyful colors because we remember that Jesus rose from the dead. When we open a plastic egg like this one *(open the egg)* and see that it is empty, it reminds us that when the women went to the tomb on Easter morning, they found that the tomb was empty. Jesus was not there!

- Hold up the plastic egg with the surprise inside. *(Keep the egg closed.)*

- **Say:** Our Bible story today tells us that when the women went to the tomb, they were surprised. Sometimes we put surprises in our Easter eggs to help us remember the surprising news that Jesus is alive.

Prepare

✓ Provide: coffee filters, different colors of food coloring, water, pencils, shallow containers, safety scissors, drinking straws, smocks, plastic tablecloth or newspapers, paper towels

✓ Pour about ¼ cup of water into the container. Add a few drops of food coloring to the water. Repeat with each color.

Prepare

✓ Provide: plastic Easter eggs; play dough or Crayola® Model Magic®; small items to place inside the eggs like tiny plastic flowers, smaller plastic eggs, small plastic birds, small plastic angel figures; 4-ounce paper cups; smocks; permanent markers

Note: You may order plastic eggs from Oriental Trading: http://www.orientaltrading.com. They have solid colored plastic eggs as well as other styles available.

NOTE: Websites are constantly changing. Although these websites were checked at the time this book was edited, we recommend that you double check the site to verify that it is still live and that it is still appropriate for children before doing the activity.

- **Say:** In the 1800's a man named Peter Karl Faberge′ created a dazzling Easter egg for the wife of the Czar of Russia. On the outside the egg looked like a regular white egg. But inside the egg was a surprise. When the egg was opened, there was an egg yolk made of gold. Inside the yolk was a gold hen with ruby eyes. More than fifty eggs were created for the royal family. Let's decorate these eggs and put surprises inside.

- Encourage the children to decorate the outside of their eggs with permanent markers.

- Have the children open their eggs.

- Let the children fill the bottom half of their eggs with play dough or Crayola® Model Magic®.

- Let the children choose from the items you have provided. Have the children stick the item into the dough.

- Or let the children create their own symbol of Easter from the Crayola® Model Magic®.

- Have the children place the top half of the egg onto the bottom half.

- Set the eggs into 4-ounce paper cups to make them sit upright.

Easter Game

- **Say:** Easter is celebrated with joy all over the world. Let's play a game that comes from Germany.

- Have the children move to an open area of the room.

- Divide the children into teams. Have the teams line up on one side of the room.

- Place a chair at the opposite side of the room for each team.

- Place two Easter baskets at the starting point for each team. Put several plastic Easter eggs in one basket for each team.

- Have the first two children from each team begin the game.

- One child runs to the chair and back.

- While the first child is running, the second child transfers (one by one) as many eggs as possible from one basket to the other basket.

- When the first child runs back to the line, the two children switch roles. The first child transfers eggs while the second child runs.

- When the second child returns, then the next two children take their turns.

- Continue the game until all the children have played.

You can find pictures of the first Faberge′ egg at: http://www.treasuresofimperialrussia.com/e_chap1_hen.html

You can find pictures of the famous Faberge′ Resurrection Egg at: http://www.treasuresofimperialrussia.com/e_chap3_resurrection.html

NOTE: Websites are constantly changing. Although these websites were checked at the time this book was edited, we recommend that you double check the site to verify that it is still live and that it is still appropriate for children before doing the activity.

Prepare
✓ Provide for each team: two Easter baskets, plastic eggs, chairs

Large Group

Bring all the children together to experience the Bible story. Tap a spoon on the side of a metal bowl or pan to alert the children to the large-group time. Use the transition activity to move the children from the interest groups to the large group area.

Egg Roll

- Have the children move to one side of the large group area.

- Use masking tape to mark a starting line in front of the children.

- Mark a finish line on the opposite side of the room.

- Give each child a plastic Easter egg.

- **Say:** Easter eggs are a symbol of new life. They help us remember that Jesus was raised from the dead.

- Explain to the children that the object of the game is to roll the Easter eggs to the finish line. However, they may only push the eggs by using their noses!

- Begin the game by saying, "Go!" Continue the game until most of the children have crossed the finish line.

Prepare

- ✓ Provide: a spoon and a metal bowl or pan

- ✓ Provide: plastic Easter eggs, masking tape

The Three Women Theater

- Have each child bring an empty Easter egg to the filling station.

- Help each child place sand, aquarium gravel, paper clips, or plastic beads inside his or her egg.

- Tape each egg shut.

- Instruct the children to sit down in your large-group area and hold their shaker eggs.

- **Say:** Today we will hear the story of the first Easter. The story takes place in a garden. In the garden there is a tomb. Three women are walking to the tomb. When you hear the word *walk* in the story, I want you to shake your eggs to make the sound of the women walking.

- Let the children get their eggs and practice.

- **Say:** Shake your eggs as if someone was walking slowly and sadly. *(Shake eggs.)* Stop! *(Stop shaking eggs.)* Shake your eggs as if you were running away from something that frightened you. *(Shake eggs.)* Stop! *(Stop shaking eggs.)*

- Tell the children the story, "Jesus Is Alive!" and encourage the children to shake their eggs as indicated in the story.

Prepare

- ✓ Provide: Bible-times costumes and containers to represent spice jars (optional)

- ✓ Provide: plastic Easter eggs; aquarium gravel, sand, paper clips, and/or plastic beads; tape

- ✓ Recruit older children, teens, or adults to play the parts of the narrator, three women, and young man.

- ✓ Photocopy the script (page 72) for the actors.

- ✓ Use the set design made earlier (page 65).

Sign the Good News

- **Say:** On Easter we celebrate the good news that Jesus is alive.

- Teach the children the signs for *Jesus* and *alive* in American Sign Language.

- **Jesus:** Touch the middle finger of the right hand to the palm of the left hand. Reverse.

- **Alive:** Make a fist with each hand with your thumb extended. Hold your fists in front of your body. Move your fists up toward your chest.

- **Say:** Say and sign "Jesus is alive!" after me—exactly like I say it.

- **Whisper:** Jesus is alive!

- **Normal voice:** Jesus is alive!

- **Shout:** Jesus is alive!

Bible Verse Game

- **Say:** Our Bible verse today is Mark 16:6: "He has been raised; he is not here."

- Have the children repeat the Bible verse.

- Have the children choose partners and stand side by side.

- Tie a piece of string or a strip of cloth around the partners' legs for a three-legged race.

- While the you are tying their legs together, have a helper hide the Easter eggs around the room.

- **Say:** Let's have an egg hunt. We have hidden eggs around the room, but you must work together with your partner to find the eggs. Each set of partners should find two eggs. Then bring the eggs back here.

- Let the children enjoy hunting for eggs.

- When each pair has found their eggs, tell the children to come back together.

- Have the children open their eggs.

- **Say:** Each of you should have one half of the Bible verse inside your egg. Untie your legs and find a new partner with the other half of the Bible verse.

- Have the children find their new partners.

- Say the Bible verse together.

- **Say:** The third day after Jesus died, God raised Jesus from the dead. Today, we celebrate the Resurrection. We have already talked about eggs as a symbol of Easter and new life.

Prepare

✓ Provide: plastic Easter eggs, string or strips of cloth for a three-legged race

✓ Photocopy the Bible verse strips (page 72). Place one strip in each egg.

Small Groups

Divide the children into small groups. You may organize the groups around age-levels or around readers and nonreaders. Keep the groups small, with a maximum of ten children in each group. You may need to have more than one of each group.

- **Ask:** What are some other symbols of Easter? *(baby animals, flowers, Easter lilies, butterflies)*

- **Say:** All of these symbols remind us that there is new life in creation. The egg reminds us of the tomb, but a baby chick comes out of an egg. A flower bulb looks dead lying in the earth, but a flower grows out of the bulb. A cocoon looks like a tomb, but a butterfly comes out of the cocoon.

- **Ask:** How do these things help us remember Easter? *(Jesus died and was buried in a tomb, but God raised him to new life.)*

- **Say:** The butterfly is a special symbol of Easter. The butterfly begins life as an egg and then becomes a caterpillar. At a certain time in its life, it spins a cocoon and sleeps. While it is inside this cocoon, it changes completely and becomes a beautiful butterfly. It starts a new life. Let's make butterflies for everyone to help us celebrate Jesus' new life.

- Have the children spread out along a table to make an assembly line. You may have as many assembly lines as the number of children permits.

- Give the first child in line a stack of the tissue paper squares. This child hands the second child one piece of tissue paper.

- Give the second child a second stack of tissue paper squares. This child takes the piece of tissue paper from the first child and adds another piece of tissue paper. (You can continue these first two steps with additional children and tissue paper rectangles). The second child gives the layered tissue paper squares to the third child.

- The third child scrunches the tissue paper together in the middle, then gives it to the fourth child.

- Give the fourth child the chenille stems. The fourth child takes the scrunched tissue paper and then twists the chenille stem around the paper to hold the "wings" in place.

- The last child takes the butterfly and makes a twist toward the ends of the chenille stem to form the antennae. This child lays the butterfly aside for later.

- Repeat until enough butterflies are made for everyone in attendance.

- Plan to use the butterflies in closing worship.

Prepare

✓ Provide: tissue paper (various colors), chenille stems, adult scissors

✓ Cut the tissue paper into squares (about 5-inch ones).

Large-Group Worship

Bring everyone together for a time of closing worship.

- Teach the children to sing "On This Joyful Easter Day" to the tune of "The Farmer in the Dell." Sing the song several times. Let the children shake their shaker eggs as they sing.

On This Joyful Easter Day

O Jesus is alive.
O Jesus is alive.
O on this joyful Easter Day,
O Jesus is alive.

- Choose a child to bring the open Bible to the front of the room. Have the child place the Bible on the altar, or stand with the Bible while the Bible verse is said.

- **Say the Bible verse together with the children:** "He has been raised; he is not here" (Mark 16:6).

- Sing the song "On This Joyful Easter Day" again. Have the children bring their butterflies to the altar or to the front of your worship area.

- Give each child a piece of clear tape.

- Have the child roll the tape and stick it to the back of a paper butterfly, tape the butterfly to the cross, and then sit back down.

- Say the following litany. Have the children say, "Hallelujah! Hallelujah!" after each statement.

Leader: There's no need to shed a tear.

Children: Hallelujah! Hallelujah!

Leader: Christ is risen. He's not here.

Children: Hallelujah! Hallelujah!

Leader: There's no need for you to fear.

Children: Hallelujah! Hallelujah!

Leader: Christ is risen. He's not here.

Children: Hallelujah! Hallelujah!

adapted from PowerXpress!® Bible Experience Stations® Mary Magdalene Story © 2005 Abingdon Press

- **Pray:** Loving God, thank you for Jesus. Thank you for the joy we feel knowing that he is alive. Amen.

- Sign *Jesus is alive!* with the children (see page 69).

Prepare

- ✓ Provide: clear tape; a large wooden cross, or a cross made from construction paper

- ✓ Place the cross in your worship area.

- ✓ Provide: a Bible

- ✓ Provide the tissue paper butterflies and shaker eggs made earlier.

Jesus Is Alive!

by Daphna Flegal

Narrator: It was very early in the morning. The sun was just beginning to rise. Three women were walking slowly and sadly to the garden. *(Shake eggs.)* Their friend Jesus was dead.

Mary Magdalene: I can't believe what happened. It was horrible.

Mary the mother of James: He was so good and loving.

Salome: They crucified him like a criminal.

Mary the mother of James: I don't know what to do.

Mary Magdalene: The only thing we can do now is take care of his body.

Salome: I hope someone can help us move the stone away from the tomb. It is too heavy for us to move by ourselves.

Narrator: The three women walked farther into the garden. Now they could see the tomb. Suddenly, they stopped in surprise. *(Stop shaking eggs.)*

Mary Magdalene: The stone . . .

Salome: . . . has been moved.

Mary the mother of James: The tomb is open!

Narrator: The three women walked carefully into the tomb. *(Shake eggs.)* Then they stopped. *(Stop shaking eggs.)* They saw a young man dressed in white. He was sitting in the tomb.

Salome: Oh, no!

Mary the mother of James: Who are you?

Mary Magdalene: God, help us!

Young Man: Don't be afraid. You are looking for Jesus. But he is not here. God raised him from the dead. Go and tell his friends. He will meet you in Galilee.

Narrator: The three women ran from the tomb. *(Shake eggs.)* They were amazed. Jesus is alive! Everyone shout it with me: "Jesus is alive!"

Everyone: Jesus is alive!

He has been raised;	he is not here.
He has been raised;	he is not here.
He has been raised;	he is not here.
He has been raised;	he is not here.

24 Hours That Changed the World (For Younger Children)